Competence to Stand Trial Evaluations

Just the Basics

Thomas Grisso, PhD
University of Massachusetts Medical School

Professional Resource Press
Sarasota, Florida

Published by
Professional Resource Press
(An imprint of Professional Resource Exchange, Inc.)
Post Office Box 3197 • Sarasota, FL 34230-3197

Printed in the United States of America

The photo on the front cover was taken in Rome, Italy by Thomas Grisso.

Cataloging-in-Publication information

Grisso, Thomas, author.
Competence to stand trial evaluations : just the basics / Thomas Grisso, PhD, University of Massachusetts Medical School.
pages cm
Includes bibliographical references.
ISBN 978-1-56887-203-2
1. Criminals--Mental health--United States. 2. Mentally ill offenders--United States. 3. Competency to stand trial--United States. 4. Insanity (Law)--United States. 5. Forensic psychiatry--United States. I. Title.
RC451.4.P68G755 2014
364.3'8--dc23

2014004852

PREFACE

This book provides clinicians a knowledge foundation for performing competence to stand trial evaluations. There are several books with that purpose, and you will find the best and most current ones listed in Appendix A. How does "Just the Basics" differ from those?

One difference is indicated in the subtitle. The book provides "the least you need to know" in order to do a creditable competence to stand trial evaluation. "Just the Basics" is fundamental, not comprehensive, and it does not offer elaborate citations to support its assertions. Knowing everything that is in this book, you will still have much to learn as you seek to improve and mature your ability to perform competence to stand trial evaluations.

Why start with this book, then, rather than going directly to more comprehensive texts? Because of its simplicity. It offers less detail and avoids many of the complexities that can arise across competence cases. So it allows you to see the forest before you start inspecting the trees.

The second way it differs from others is its organization. Many years ago I developed a way to conceptualize all legal competencies as having five components in common (Grisso, 1986, 2003). "Just the Basics" uses these concepts throughout the book as its organizing framework for thinking about "five objectives" for competence to stand trial evaluations.

I wrote a book for Professional Resource Press similar to this one almost 25 years ago. Some of the material from that book is included here. But 25 years produced a great deal more research on defendant's competence to stand trial and competence evaluations. Most of that research is not described here, although it is reflected in the guidance the book offers. Almost all of the structured competence assessment tools described in Chapter 3 were developed in the past 25 years. Competence to stand trial was not applied in juvenile courts until the late 1990s, but now competence evaluations of juveniles are routine. This book includes numerous discussions of how juvenile competence evaluations differ from competence evaluations of adults.

Other changes are the result of my own experiences during those 25 years. Since then I have taught postdoctoral forensic psychology fellows every year, helped develop and monitor standards for competence evaluations for the state of Massachusetts, provided consultation to many other states to develop their competence evaluation standards, and chaired the faculty that evaluates forensic reports submitted to the American Board of Forensic Psychology for national board-certification in forensic psychology. All of this led me to some discussions that I would not have thought to provide in my earlier book on this topic. It has been just as interesting to discover what has not changed. The "five objective" model that I developed in the 1980s works as well now as it did then, despite all the changes in the field. The legal standard for competence to stand trial has been given new interpretations, but the standard itself—offered in *Dusky v. U.S.* in 1960—continues to be applied nationwide. Many issues and errors in competence evaluations are just as relevant today (and sometimes just as frequent) as they were in the early days of forensic psychology and psychiatry.

"Just the Basics" is written primarily for the practicing forensic clinician and for students with that aspiration. During the drafting and revision, I found myself speaking to the reader in the style of a supervision or consultation session more than a textbook or manual.

When I wrote the earlier book that formed the basis for this one, it was part of a project for which I received a research grant (#MH-37231) from the Antisocial and Violent Behavior Branch of the National Institute of Mental Health. The AVB Branch no longer exists. At that time it was directed by Saleem Shah, a man whose thinking and mentoring were among the greatest influences on the early development of the fields of psychology and law as well as forensic psychology practice. It was at his insistence that I attempted the earlier version.

In my earlier attempt I depended on the seasoned wisdom of professionals like Norm Poythress and Jerry Serafino to guide my writing. (Thanks again, both of you.) Since then, a major source of knowledge and inspiration has been the "faculty" of the Practice Sample Review Committee, a dozen ABFP board-certified clinicians who review forensic reports (many of them competence evaluations) submitted by candidates for certification. As Chair of this committee for many years, I benefited greatly from discussions with these thoughtful and dedicated forensic colleagues, and I thank them one and all. And finally, thanks to Dr. Lawrence Ritt and the crew at Professional Resource Press for their continued support.

Thomas Grisso
Shrewsbury, Massachusetts

TABLE OF CONTENTS

GETTING STARTED

This book is a practical guide that summarizes basic concepts and methods for performing evaluations of defendants' competence to stand trial. It aims to help mental health professionals perform competence to stand trial evaluations that satisfy three broad requirements:

- To provide information to courts that is of greatest relevance for their legal decisions
- To meet scientific and practice standards
- To comply with ethical standards of mental health professionals

"Just the Basics" is designed to provide only that which is basic and essential for beginning forensic evaluation practice. It describes "the least you need to know" for purposes of understanding how to perform creditable competence evaluations. The reading-time for the text is about 3.5 to 5 hours.

THE READERS

The book is aimed at several types of users:

- Practicing clinical psychologists and psychiatrists who are re-tooling to add forensic assessments to their practice
- Participants in workshops on competence evaluations for which a very basic reference will fit the time and budget of the instructor and learners
- Psychology graduate students, psychiatry residents, and post-doctoral forensic mental health fellows who are in training for performing forensic assessments

- Psychology and criminal justice undergraduates who may go on to graduate training that would prepare them for these evaluations
- Attorneys who seek a basic standard that shows what they should expect, at minimum, from competence to stand trial evaluations

Legal scholars, behavioral science researchers, and advanced forensic clinicians are less likely to find this book sufficiently detailed to meet their needs. Its legal citations and references to research are highly selective. More comprehensive and detailed analyses of competence to stand trial evaluations can be found in the references in Appendix A.

THE BOOK'S CONCEPTUAL APPROACH

The author's projects in earlier years created a way of conceptualizing all legal competencies as having five components in common. They are labeled Functional, Causal, Interactive, Conclusory and Dispositional. These concepts are used throughout "Just the Basics" to form "five objectives" of competence to stand trial evaluations. They are used to organize everything from the design of a competence evaluation to the collection and interpretation of the data.

THE BOOK'S ORGANIZATION

The book has seven chapters and several appendixes. The first six chapters follow the sequence of the assessment process from beginning to end. The seventh chapter goes beyond the assessment process to discuss ways that legal systems and institutions in which examiners conduct forensic evaluations can have an impact on their competence evaluations and reports. The Appendices provide a variety of supplemental information cited in the seven chapters (e.g., annotated references to relevant books and journals, and details of certain assessment methods).

USING "JUST THE BASICS"

This book is intended especially for use in training programs—continuing education workshops, classrooms, seminars, or professional academic settings—although it is equally suited for the individual professional studying outside these formal arrangements. When used in these contexts, the information in the book must be supplemented by the following types of information and experience in order to implement the procedures that the book describes.

MODELING AND EXPERIENTIAL LEARNING

The process of learning any clinical activity involves three stages: (a) acquiring understanding of the relevant definitions, concepts, and methods; (b) exposure to cases so that understanding can be "rehearsed" and applied to various case circumstances; and (c) performance of cases with some input from a clinician who is experienced in the clinical activity that is being learned.

Most of "Just the Basics" provides only the understanding in the first stage of this process. Practice in applying this understanding, and experience in performing competence evaluations, require that the reader gain consultation and supervision. For graduate students and postdoctoral fellows, this occurs in the course of their formal training. For independent professionals, ways to obtain this experience are described in Chapter 7.

LEARNING THE LOCAL RULES AND PROCEDURES

Information in this book must be supplemented with the applicable legal definitions and procedural requirements in one's own jurisdiction. These requirements differ from state to state, and the book was not designed to cover the specific differences across jurisdictions. The definitions and procedures the book describes were selected for their general application across the widest range of states and jurisdictions, but they might apply only imperfectly in some jurisdictions.

Workshop trainers usually will provide the necessary information specific to one's own jurisdiction. In addition, some states' Offices of

Mental Health or Forensic Mental Health often are prepared to respond to professionals' requests for information about the state's laws and procedures for competence evaluations.

CONTINUING YOUR EDUCATION

Mental health professionals have an obligation to keep themselves informed of new developments in their field of practice. This obligation is especially important when approaching any type of forensic practice. Appendix A provides annotated references for recent books that discuss many of the definitions, issues, and methods in this book in considerably more detail. It also lists several professional journals that frequently publish research reports and discussions of new developments relevant to competence assessments.

TAKING RESPONSIBILITY

No book can tell a professional exactly how to perform any clinical task. It can offer definitions, provide guidelines, recommend methods, and suggest strategies. Yet were you to follow the procedures described here to the letter, this would not ensure quality practice and in certain cases might even jeopardize it. In the end, professionals must make their own individual judgments concerning how and when the book's recommendations are to be applied. Often this will depend on the specific demands of one's own work setting and the circumstances of individual cases.

"Just the Basics" is simple and logically structured. It clearly favors certain methods, but it is not a cookbook. Point-by-point adherence to these recommendations is less important than gaining an appreciation of the legal demands, issues, and objectives that the book's approach seeks to satisfy. With that appreciation, you will be in an informed position to be responsible for final judgments about how to perform competence evaluations that meet basic practice standards.

Chapter 1

LEGAL DEFINITION OF COMPETENCE TO STAND TRIAL

Designing pretrial evaluations of competence to stand trial begins with a clear idea of the questions that the court is asking. Without clarity about the referral question, you cannot decide meaningfully what data to collect, and you will not arrive at an opinion that answers the court's questions. This chapter defines the questions as the law proposes them. Chapter 2 translates those questions with forensic concepts that bridge the gap between law and your competence evaluation.

The primary reason for competence to stand trial evaluations is to *provide courts with relevant information when making a legal decision about a defendant's capacity to participate in a trial.* The key word is "relevant." Many things that are relevant for other types of clinical and forensic mental health evaluations are not relevant for competence evaluations. The court's decision about a defendant's competence is not informed by a general psychological evaluation aimed at treatment plans, or by forensic evaluations that address the defendant's dangerousness. The purpose of a competence evaluation is fulfilled only if it is designed to address concepts related to the legal standard for competence to stand trial.

This chapter begins by explaining the need for the competence to stand trial doctrine in criminal and juvenile courts. We then review critical legal definitions of competence to stand trial found in statutes and a number of legal cases. Citations for the relevant legal cases are in Appendix B, along with brief notes about what the cases contribute to the definition of competence to stand trial. Appendix B also includes a number of other legal competence cases not described in this chapter but which you might want to consult after you understand the basics.

THE REASON FOR THE COMPETENCE DOCTRINE

The American system of criminal law adopted the doctrine of competence to stand trial from English common law. At least as early as the 17th century, courts were concerned about the ability of deaf, mute, or "lunatic" defendants to participate meaningfully in their trials. Why would law and society be concerned about this?

The first reason is to assure *fairness to the individual* in the criminal trial process. An adversarial trial system in a democracy values individuals' rights to freedom and autonomy. This requires that the accused has a fair opportunity to mount any reasonable, available defense against the charges brought by the state. This opportunity is threatened when mental incapacities seriously reduce the defendant's ability to make decisions about a defense and to meet other demands of the defendant's role in a trial. To allow the defendant to proceed to trial under such circumstances would threaten the fairness of the trial process.

A second reason for the legal concept is to *maintain the integrity of the justice system*. Trying people with serious mental impairments is not only unfair to the person, but also runs the risk of reducing the public's respect for a system that does not protect a citizen from that unfairness.

Third, the legal concept of competence to stand trial promotes the *accuracy of information* in the trial. A defendant who is disadvantaged by mental incapacities might not recognize the relevance of certain information for the trial, and the defendant might have knowledge about facts relevant for the trial that others do not have. This would deprive the court of potentially important information and perhaps would lead in some cases to wrong conclusions.

Competence to stand trial is only one of several legal competencies. Civil and juvenile law contain many others, such as competence to care for self and property (in guardianship cases) and competence to consent to or refuse treatment. Criminal law itself has other competencies (e.g., competence to be executed). Moreover, the legal definitions of these competencies differ in various ways, so much so that a given person at a given moment, with a particular mental disability, may be legally competent for one of those purposes and not for another.

We will discuss the implications of this at various points in this chapter. For now, the important observation is that legal competencies are *specific* competencies. A competence to stand trial evaluation will not serve to address a court's questions about other legal competencies because it is designed to address the legal questions that are specific to competence to stand trial.

Throughout this book we will refer to "competence to stand trial" evaluations simply as "competence evaluations" without the "to stand trial" modifier. This is simply for ease of reading. It does not imply that the evaluations we are describing would serve for evaluations involving other legal competencies.

SOURCES OF LAW DEFINING COMPETENCE TO STAND TRIAL

A competence to stand trial evaluation is designed in accord with the law's definition of competence to stand trial, as well as its rules for legal procedures that the court follows in arriving at competence decisions. You must know these laws that are the focus of your evaluation. They will be found in one or more of three sources.

One source is your state's *statutes*, which offer two types of definitions: (a) the state's definition of incompetence to stand trial, often called the "standard" for competence to stand trial; and (b) rules defining the legal process for determining whether a defendant's circumstances meet that standard. Consulting your state's statutes, you will find that there are many questions they do not answer. Statutes often are crafted with broad brush strokes because judges must apply them to cases with wide-ranging differences in specific facts and conditions.

The second source is *case law*. As courts apply the statutes to individual cases, their decisions themselves become law that guides other courts' interpretations in subsequent, similar cases. This process of the dynamic evolution of law through adherence to precedent in decisions in similar cases is called *stare decisis*. The most important cases that define the contours of a state's competence laws are those that have been appealed to one of the state's higher courts. This typically happens because of an attorney's challenge to a lower court's interpretation of the state's competence laws. To know how competence is defined in your state, you must be aware of the more important appellate competence to stand trial decisions in your state. In addition, some federal cases have established competence laws that every state must follow.

The third source is *administrative regulations.* These are rules that may have been published by a state's office of courts, or by a department of mental health if it is authorized to regulate forensic evaluations in the state. Administrative rules often define details of the competence process not covered by statute or case law. Those details may include, for example, how a court makes a referral to a mental health professional once it has decided to order a competence evaluation, or what qualifications a professional must have to be authorized to perform the evaluation.

Laws from all three of these sources differ considerably from state to state. This manual cannot identify all of these differences or the details associated with administrative regulations. The following discussions must be sufficiently general to be applicable across states. You must use local resources to discover the specific laws that apply in your own state.

THE LEGAL STANDARD FOR COMPETENCE TO STAND TRIAL

The "legal standard" for competence to stand trial refers to the definition of competence that the court must apply when deciding about a defendant's competence. As you verify this definition in your own state, you may find that your state's statutes do not use the term "competence to stand trial." Common variations include "fitness to stand trial," "fitness to proceed," and "competence to proceed." In secondary sources you might also encounter the term "adjudicative competence," a term that has arisen primarily in scholarly treatises but is less often found in statutes or case law.

THE DUSKY *STANDARD*

Almost every state employs a legal definition of competence to stand trial patterned after the definition given by the U.S. Supreme Court in *Dusky v. United States* (1960):

> [T]he test must be whether he [the defendant] has sufficient present ability to consult with his attorney with a reasonable degree of rational understanding and a rational as well as factual understanding of the proceedings against him. (p. 402)

Some states use the exact wording of *Dusky*. Others have abbreviated some phrases or made slight changes to the wording. Almost all, however, retain the essential concepts: "consult with attorney" and "rational (and) factual understanding of the proceedings."

Most states' statutes do not provide much further guidance about how competence is defined, although a few offer definitions of the *Dusky* abilities. For example, Florida's statute (Fla. R. Crim. P. sec. 3.21[a]) directs the court to consider a number of capacities:

1. Appreciate the charges or allegations against him;
2. Appreciate the range and nature of possible penalties, if applicable, which may be imposed in the proceedings against him;
3. Understand the adversary nature of the legal process;
4. Disclose to his attorney facts pertinent to the proceedings at issue;
5. Manifest appropriate courtroom behavior;
6. Testify relevantly.

Some states have added the requirement that deficiencies in the abilities noted in the *Dusky* standard must be due to certain conditions. The most common conditions use labels like "mental disorder" or "mental disease or defect." Developmental disability (mental retardation) almost always is included. In most states, however, one must go to case law or regulations to identify these further. States vary in their definitions of a "mental disorder" or "mental disease or defect" for purposes of competence to stand trial. In addition, the majority of states, by statute or case law, now recognize "developmental immaturity" as a potential reason for deficits related to incompetence to stand trial in cases heard in juvenile court. (Competence in juvenile cases is discussed later.)

UNITY OF THE LEGAL CONCEPT OF COMPETENCE TO STAND TRIAL

Prior to the 1990s, there was sometimes disagreement between jurisdictions on whether defendants might be found competent for certain tasks in the trial process but not for others. For example, imagine that a defendant is able to grasp what is necessary to make a plea, but is unable to testify if the defendant's testimony is needed during a future trial. Could defendants be found competent for the first purpose but, if they pled not guilty, found incompetent to proceed to the trial hearing?

Could a defendant be found "competent to proceed with counsel," but possibly not competent to decide to waive the right to counsel?

Guidance on this matter was provided by the U.S. Supreme Court in *Godinez v. Moran* (1993). The Court decided that (a) one must be competent for all stages and for all possible decisions that might arise in the trial process, and (b) decision-making capacities are basic for exercising the functions outlined in the *Dusky* standard.

Some defendants indicate their intention to dismiss counsel and represent themselves. Does this mean defendants must be found incompetent if they would not have sufficient capacities to represent themselves? No, the U.S. Supreme Court decided in *Indiana v. Edwards* (2008). Defendants need to have sufficient decisional capacity to *decide* whether to exercise their basic right to waive counsel and represent themselves if they choose. However, they might later be found unable to actually have the capacities to represent themselves. This latter question—could the defendant actually manage the task of self-representation in a trial—is not part of the competence to stand trial inquiry.

COMPETENCE IN JUVENILE COURT

Competence to stand trial has increased in its application in juvenile courts since the mid-1990s (Grisso, 1997). Before that time, most states considered it unnecessary for young people to be competent to stand trial in juvenile court. *In re Gault* (1967) had afforded young people many of the same rights in juvenile court as applied to adults in criminal court, including the right to be represented by legal counsel. But the right to be competent to stand trial did not evolve in the two decades after *Gault*. Possibly this was because states believed that representation by legal counsel—in a system that was intended to operate "in the best interest of the child"—was enough, so that a juvenile who was an autonomous participant in the trial was not necessary.

This changed, however, when the U.S. underwent a period in the early 1990s during which most states developed new laws pertaining to delinquency, in response to what was considered a wave of more serious and lethal crimes by juveniles (Grisso, 1996; Grisso & Schwartz, 2000). These laws greatly increased penalties, decreased leniency, increased the number of youth who were transferred for trial in criminal court, and included some juvenile court sentencing schemes that carried well into young people's adult years. As a consequence, beginning in the middle-1990s, attorneys representing young people in juvenile court began to raise the question of competence to stand trial with increasing frequency. Within a few years, requests for competence to stand trial evaluations in juvenile court increased from almost none in the mid-1990s to hundreds annually in most urban areas of the U.S. (Grisso, 2005).

Until recently there was little legal guidance about how competence to stand trial should be applied in juvenile court. But recent legislation and case law have begun to create some consensus (Larson & Grisso, 2012). All states but one have laws that recognize competence to stand trial in juvenile court. Moreover, a growing number of states (about one-third by 2012) have separate statutes and case law for competence to stand trial in juvenile court rather than applying their criminal statutes' provisions.

In general, states employ the same *Dusky* standard used in their criminal courts. However, a significant number of states specifically recognize that youths may be incompetent to stand trial for reasons other than mental illness or developmental disability—specifically, developmental immaturity (e.g., Arizona in *In re Hyrum*, 2006; California in *Timothy J. v. Sacramento County*, 2007; Michigan in *In re Carey*, 2000). A few states instruct juvenile courts to judge youths' competence according to "adolescent norms" (that is, comparing them to their peers) rather than requiring a comparison to the capacities of adults. This means that the *Dusky* standard would still be used, but a youth in juvenile court might not have to demonstrate the same level or degree of *Dusky* abilities as would be required for an adult in criminal court.

States with juvenile competence statutes also make some procedural provisions that are different than in criminal court: for example, regarding the qualifications of forensic examiners appropriate for assessing adolescents, or differences in disposition if the youth is found incompetent. You should consult Larson and Grisso (2012) and Kruh and Grisso (2009) for these differences in application of the competence concept in juvenile courts.

THE LEGAL PROCESS FOR COMPETENCE TO STAND TRIAL

The legal definition of competence to stand trial comes into play at each of several critical stages in the process of a competence case. Each of these stages is guided by procedural rules also found variably in statutes, case law, or administrative regulations. They often provide guidance about how evaluations should be performed.

RAISING THE QUESTION

The question of a defendant's competence can be raised whenever there is a "*bona fide* doubt" about the defendant's competence (*Drope v. Missouri*, 1975). The degree of doubt does not need to be substantial. Any court officer (judge, prosecutor, defense attorney) may raise the question, although it is most often the defense attorney. Sometimes defense counsel seeks an independent competence evaluation (covered under attorney-client privilege). But in the great majority of cases, the question is raised to the court, and the court orders the competence evaluation. This suspends further progress of the case until the evaluation is performed and a competence decision is reached.

The question can be raised at any stage in the proceeding. It can be raised at the earliest stage (e.g., arraignment) or in the midst of a formal hearing to adjudicate the alleged offense. Moreover, if a defendant is found competent and the case proceeds, the question can be raised again at any time that there is a "*bone fide* doubt" about the defendant's competence. This recognizes that some defendant's mental conditions might change in the course of a lengthy trial process.

Examiners receiving court orders to perform competence evaluations should not assume that the defendant is "probably incompetent" merely because an evaluation has been ordered. In fact, only about 20% of defendants referred for competence evaluations are found incompetent after the evaluation (but with considerable variation across jurisdictions, as reviewed by Zapf & Roesch, 2009). There are several reasons why the incompetence rate is low. Sometimes even vague suggestions (e.g., that the defendant was once psychiatrically hospitalized) or minimal signs of disability may be sufficient to order an evaluation. In addition, attorneys sometimes request competence evaluations not because they are deeply concerned about the defendant's abilities, but for tactical reasons (e.g., to obtain information that might be useful later in developing an argument for mitigation in sentencing). The mere fact that the question is raised, therefore, tells one little about the likelihood that the defendant is incompetent.

THE EVALUATION

Statutes rarely describe precisely how the evaluation must be performed. Most, however, describe who can perform it, where, and how much time is allowed.

Many states require special qualifications for examiners who are employed by the state to perform court-ordered forensic evaluations. Usually they include qualified psychiatrists and psychologists with doctoral degrees and appropriate training and experience to perform forensic competence evaluations in criminal cases. Sometimes professionals taking such evaluations on court order must meet annual continuing education requirements to be eligible as a competence examiner. A few states require more than one examiner (e.g., Arizona, Florida, Hawaii) for all or most competence cases (typically performing their evaluations independently). Some states have different qualifications for examiners who perform competence evaluations of juveniles, such as child clinical specialization. (See Chapter 7 for further discussion of examiner qualifications.)

All states have provisions for evaluating defendants in psychiatric hospitals, and most states also allow competence evaluations to be performed when defendants are in jail or residing in the community. Often they require the latter unless the defendant's mental condition and risk of harm require hospitalization (a provision that is guided by the legal concept of "least restrictive alternative").

Finally, most states' statutes limit the time between the order and completion of the evaluation. Common time frames are 20, 30 or 40 days, but some states allow as little as 10 days and as many as 60 days.

HEARING ON COMPETENCE

When the examiner's report is sent to the court, typically the court will make it available to both attorneys in the case. If they stipulate (agree) to the examiner's opinion, the examiner is unlikely to be asked to provide testimony, and the court is very likely to make a finding of competence or incompetence on the basis of the report alone. If the question needs to be argued, the examiner is likely to be asked to provide oral testimony. Courts vary a great deal in their readiness to accept examiners' opinions concerning whether the defendant should be found competent or incompetent, some doing so almost always and others far less consistently.

DISPOSITION FOR INCOMPETENCE FINDINGS

If the court finds the defendant competent, the case proceeds to pretrial and trial matters. If the defendant is found incompetent to stand trial, the court must make a dispositional decision—that is, decide what will be done with the defendant. The primary question at this point is whether the defendant's deficits can be altered so that competent participation is possible in the future. This is often called "restoration of competence," but this book refers to it as "remediation." The term "restoration" arose historically in the context of incompetence due to serious episodes of mental illness, so that the treatment objective was to "restore" people to their prepsychotic state. But many defendants—for example, persons with serious and pervasive intellectual disabilities, or some juveniles who have not yet matured cognitively—may be incompetent due to conditions that are not episodic They may never have had the capacities that competence requires. Therefore, remediation is a more meaningful term for efforts to help defendants gain competence to participate in their trials.

Either by law or practice, there are five things that courts need to consider when addressing the competence remediation question:

- Is the nature of the defendant's incompetence potentially *remediable*?
- If so, *what intervention* is most likely to succeed for this defendant?
- *Where* can that intervention best be accomplished?
- Given that intervention, what is the *likelihood that remediation will succeed*—that is, will allow the defendant to meet competence criteria?
- Within what *period of time* is this likely to be accomplished?

Note that the objective of remediation is not to provide a regimen of treatment that will allow the individual to function better in everyday life. The focus is specifically on reducing symptoms or increasing cognitive functioning that is necessary to satisfy the *Dusky* standard.

These questions must be answered because of a ruling by the U.S. Supreme Court in *Jackson v. Indiana* (1972) that influenced all states' laws. States may not allow a defendant to be held under criminal charges for purposes of treatment to remediate incompetence if (a) their condition is not remediable or (b) they cannot be remediated within a reasonable period of time. Most states' statutes, therefore, provide limits on the amount of time that a person may be treated to remediate incompetence.

REMEDIATION AND REEVALUATION

Most states order reevaluations of competence periodically during the remediation process. They also require periodic reports back to the court of jurisdiction. If these reports eventually lead to the conclusion that the defendant's condition is not remediable, or that it cannot be accomplished by the time limit for incompetence remediation, most states provide that defendants cannot continue to be held under the criminal complaint. Their criminal or delinquency charges must be dismissed. However, courts in most states have the authority to commit the individual as a civil psychiatric patient if the individual meets the state's civil commitment criteria. Typically those criteria include serious mental illness and danger to the community or to the individual's own welfare.

COMMON MISCONCEPTIONS ABOUT COMPETENCE TO STAND TRIAL

Forensic examiners and legal professionals sometimes demonstrate misunderstandings and misconceptions of competence to stand trial. They are manifested less frequently in recent years, but they are worth describing so that you can recognize them if they arise.

COMPETENCE AND MENTAL ILLNESS

You may sometimes hear incompetence described as though the presence of mental illness is the equivalent of incompetence. Incompetence and mental illness are not synonymous. Notice that the *Dusky* definition of competence refers to "ability." Legal interpretations of this term leave no doubt that the mere presence of mental illness alone—even severe mental illness—does not answer the questions of "ability" asked by the *Dusky* definition. A defendant may be psychotic, developmentally disabled, or developmentally immature yet still be competent to stand trial. The central question is what the defendant actually understands, believes, or can do related to the *Dusky* definition. In most courts, many defendants will be found competent to stand trial even if they have mental disorders that require hospitalization, often because the degree of their symptoms does not seem to be interfering with their abilities related to the *Dusky* definition.

Sometimes states require that incompetence must be due to some particular condition (e.g., mental illness). This does not change the above fact. It simply means that a defendant without the specified mental condition cannot be found incompetent. But a defendant with that condition may or may not be competent.

There is an important message here for examiners. As we will describe later, providing a formal diagnosis and description of a defendant's symptoms is a central objective of a competence evaluation, but it is never a *sufficient* objective. Similarly, if a state allows juveniles to be found incompetent due to developmental immaturity, merely identifying the ways in which the youth is developmentally immature will miss the point. Some developmentally immature youths are nevertheless competent to stand trial, depending on their actual abilities associated with the *Dusky* standard.

COMPETENCE AND CRIMINAL RESPONSIBILITY

You may sometimes hear these terms used interchangeably. They are entirely separate legal concepts. The *Dusky* definition refers to *present* ability. Criminal responsibility refers to ability or mental state *at the time of the offense* (relevant for a finding of "not guilty by reason of insanity"). Moreover, the two legal concepts refer to very different abilities. Competence and criminal responsibility are two separate questions, and examiners should address only the question that is asked rather than answering both questions whenever either of them is asked.

LEGAL COMPETENCE AND THE COMPETENCE EVALUATION

You may find that judges or attorneys sometimes presume that the court cannot find a defendant incompetent if the forensic examiner's opinion did not support that conclusion. A forensic examiner's opinion in no way binds the court's decision. It provides evidence that the court considers. While the examiner's evidence is being presented, the data may be challenged in court, the logic will be scrutinized, and the court may have other evidence that the examiner's report does not provide. For these and other reasons, courts can—and sometimes do—conclude quite the opposite of the examiner's opinion about competence or incompetence.

COMPETENCE AND THE ADJUDICATION PROCESS

At different times in history, the legal concept of competence to stand trial has been mistakenly identified with individuals' competence to do what is necessary in a formal hearing at which evidence is heard and argued before a judge. This is a mistaken notion based on a narrow definition of "trial." The trial to which the competence doctrine refers is the whole trial process—all important stages of the adjudication from arraignment to defendant-attorney consultations to the formal trial and sentencing. In part this is why legal scholars in recent years have coined the term "adjudicative competence" as a more accurate description of the focus of competence to stand trial. This acknowledges that competence means the ability to participate in the full range of events during the adjudicative process. This makes sense also because most defendants—about 90%—never have a formal trial during which they participate in a hearing on the evidence. They plead guilty, often as a part of a plea agreement. And competence is just as important for that decision as for participation in a formal trial.

In summary, the law's definition of competence to stand trial defines the "referral question" for competence evaluations. Yet our ability to address the question requires more clarification than the law provides. What specific abilities and other characteristics of the defendant do we need to be able to describe to satisfy the *Dusky* standard? And how can we best frame the referral question so that it provides guidance for our data collection? These questions are the focus of Chapter 2.

Chapter 2

FORENSIC CONCEPTS TO GUIDE COMPETENCE EVALUATIONS

Forensic psychology and psychiatry have developed a rich source of concepts to frame and structure a competence to stand trial evaluation. They offer a translation of the law's concerns into things that are observable, sometimes measurable, and compatible with clinical and psychological concepts regarding human behavior and disability.

This chapter offers a five-concept package for framing that translation. The concepts are related to *five primary objectives* of competence evaluations: the *Functional, Causal, Interactive, Conclusory,* and *Dispositional* objectives. The concepts were developed in a project that was reported in a book, *Evaluating Competencies* (Grisso, 1986; revised in 2003), which used the concepts to describe five components that all legal competencies—criminal, civil, and juvenile—have in common. They were then applied to each legal competence to identify key objectives of forensic evaluations for those competencies. Today they continue to be cited in major texts that offer a framework for thinking about competence to stand trial as a forensic concept that bridges the law and the examiner's evaluation task.

THE FUNCTIONAL OBJECTIVE

The competence evaluation should describe the defendant's strengths and deficits in the functional abilities to which the legal standard for competence to stand trial refers.

This is called the *Functional objective* because the evaluation should focus on the defendant's current functioning as it relates to the adjudicative process. The functional abilities relevant for competence to stand trial are different from the general psychological abilities that often form the focus of clinical evaluations—that is, general intelligence, memory, or capacities for abstract reasoning. Instead the Functional objective requires describing *what the defendant does or does not understand and believe about the trial process, what the defendant is or is not able to do in that process, and the defendant's reasoning about trial-related matters.* Thus a competence evaluation always requires direct assessment of defendants' actual knowledge of adjudicative events and what they believe specifically about their own trial process. Chapter 3 will examine various methods for assessing functional competence abilities.

TYPES OF COMPETENCE ABILITIES

Recall that the phrases in the *Dusky* standard that define these abilities are general and therefore vague. The examiner needs more specific guidance about the things that defendants are expected to be able to do in the trial process and in client-attorney interactions. A number of lists of specific functional abilities related to competence to stand trial have been developed, beginning in the 1960s and continuing to the present. Appendix C offers a number of these lists. They have much in common, including a tendency to group functions similarly:

(a) defendant's understanding of the basic purpose and process of criminal trials;
(b) defendant's abilities associated with consulting and assisting counsel; and
(c) defendant's ability to apply information to his or her own trial circumstances (rational use of what one understands when applied to one's participation in the trial process).

THE "FACTUAL" AND "RATIONAL" UNDERSTANDING CONCEPTS

A helpful way to conceptualize the functional abilities for competence is to think of them according to *Dusky's* terms referring to "factual" and "rational" understanding. *Factual understanding* refers to basic knowledge. For example, a defendant who knows that judges make sure the law is applied correctly to a case have a factual understanding of that role of the judge. In contrast, *rational understanding* refers to the ability to apply knowledge to one's own situation. For example, the same defendant in the above example—while clearly understanding what a judge is supposed to do—might nevertheless have a delusional belief that the judge in his or her own case is part of a global conspiracy to find the defendant guilty. This belief is an example of failure to understand rationally.

THE "UARC" CONCEPTS

A further refinement in conceptualizing relevant functional abilities for competence is offered by a set of four organizing concepts: Understanding, Appreciation, Reasoning, and Communication (UARC). The first three of these concepts arose as a consequence of theoretical and empirical research during the past 20 years (e.g., see Grisso & Appelbaum, 1998; Poythress et al., 2002). The fourth has been added to capture some features of competence that most schemes recognize but less often have been the subject of specific research.

Understanding

In this conceptual scheme, Understanding is synonymous with "factual" understanding described in the earlier discussion of factual and rational understanding. If a defendant can describe the basic functions of a defense attorney (supposed to help you, argues for you in court, is on your side), the defendant has factual understanding of the role of defense counsel.

Appreciation

Appreciation refers to the defendant's ability to appreciate the significance of what the defendant factually understands when applied to the defendant's own situation. For example, the defendant knows what attorneys do, but believes that her own attorney will not do it because he is the devil. Common reasons for failure of Appreciation are fixed false beliefs (e.g., delusions or rigid perceptions associated with some cases of serious mood disorders). Among adolescents, failure of Appreciation also can be related to developmentally immature ways of interpreting the relevance of what one knows. For example, one may fail to appreciate that attorneys defend people even if they have committed the alleged offense—often seen in adolescents when they have not yet formed the ability to master abstract concepts.

Reasoning

Reasoning refers to the ability to process information logically. Some defendants (e.g., because of developmental disability) may have acceptable Understanding and adequate Appreciation, yet fail to be able to process a decision—for example, a plea agreement—that requires weighing multiple pros and cons of two or three options.

You will find some variation in the field regarding how the Reasoning concept is used. Sometimes it refers to processing information, as described above. But you will also hear it used synonymously with "decision making abilities." Decision making, of course, is an important role of the defendant. Earlier we noted that the U.S. Supreme Court in *Godinez v. Moran* (1993) highlighted this as an important part of competence to stand trial. But I recommend thinking of decision making as a function that is influenced by all three types of abilities that we have just reviewed. For example, when reviewing a defendant's decision making about a plea bargain, you might find that it is impaired by a misunderstanding of the meaning of guilty or not-guilty pleas (Understanding) or by difficulties in processing the complexities of the decision (Reasoning). Or both of those functions may be intact, but the defendant's delusional beliefs about the situation (Appreciation) cause the individual to reach a conclusion that is distorted by those beliefs. In this approach, the quality of the defendant's "decision making" is potentially a consequence of deficits in any of the three primary concepts we've reviewed here.

Communication

Some aspects of the defendant's abilities to receive and send communications are not captured well in the previous three concepts. The Communications concept focuses on the ability to receive information and make oneself understood by others in the role of defendant. The concept is most closely related to the part of the *Dusky* standard regarding "ability to consult with his attorney," which means more than "being able to talk to your lawyer." It refers to participation in the defense for which the attorney is responsible. In that context, defendants must be able to convey their thoughts to others and manage their behavior in ways that do not disadvantage their defense. Sometimes defendants' emotional or cognitive capacities create substantial difficulties in working with their attorneys, tolerating court hearings, or being able to testify if necessary.

THE CAUSAL OBJECTIVE

The evaluation should provide information that suggests the cause of any deficits in competence abilities that have been observed.

This fulfills the *Causal objective* of the evaluation, allowing the examiner to explain the most plausible reason for the deficits encountered in the Functional portion of the evaluation, as well as other possible but less plausible causes. This Causal information is legally relevant because certain reasons for defendants' deficits in competence abilities essentially do not qualify them for a finding of incompetence.

There are seven common reasons for observed deficits in functional abilities in competence cases. Three of them are causes of deficits that can lead to incompetence findings, three usually do not allow for a finding of incompetence, and one offers complexities that make the outcome less predictable.

CAUSES ALLOWING FOR A FINDING OF INCOMPETENCE

The most common causes of functional deficits in incompetence cases are (a) *mental illness,* (b) *developmental disability (mental retardation),* and (c) *developmental immaturity.* Repeating earlier cautions, this does not mean that all persons with these conditions are incompetent. It means that if they have serious deficits in their functional competence abilities that are a consequence of these conditions, they may be found incompetent to stand trial.

Regarding mental illnesses, symptoms of psychotic disorders offer the most frequent explanations for deficits in competence abilities among defendants found incompetent to stand trial. Other important disorders, however, include Major Depression, various neurological disorders, and amnestic disorders (both organic and psychogenic). The formal diagnosis is less important than the connection between the symptoms and the deficits, as well as showing that the symptoms are related to some mental disorder.

Developmental disabilities often impair the individual's ability to understand trial-relevant information or to engage in cognitive tasks required for meaningful decision making regarding waiver of rights and pleading. Similarly, a youth's developmental immaturity may impair ability to understand, appreciate, or reason about trial-related matters because various necessary cognitive abilities may simply not have yet developed.

CAUSES TYPICALLY NOT ALLOWING FOR A FINDING OF INCOMPETENCE

Another three common reasons for observed deficits in functional competence abilities are (d) *ignorance of the legal process,* (e) *situational states,* and (f) *dissimulation of deficits.* Typically, if poor functional performance on competence abilities is related to these causes, the defendant will not be found incompetent to stand trial (absent any of the first three conditions discussed above).

Regarding *ignorance of the legal process,* lack of knowledge of trial-related matters can be a result of simple lack of exposure to such information in the past. For example, a defendant recently may have arrived from another country with a culture that does not resolve legal questions according to the adversarial process used in U.S. courts. Lack of knowledge often can be easily remedied if the defendant's psychological resources do not offer remarkable barriers to learning from simple instruction.

Situational conditions refer to states like fatigue, or an emotional reaction to a piece of bad news, that can temporarily impair a person's performance at the time of evaluation. It can also refer to external situations that impair performance, such as an evaluation performed under distracting conditions.

Dissimulation in competence evaluations comes in two forms, both of which are an individual's attempt to appear other than they are, typically to gain some personal benefit associated with a finding of incompetence to stand trial. Some defendants dissimulate poor performance during the inquiry into their functional competence-related abilities. Others dissimulate the causes of functional deficits—that is, symptoms of mental illness or developmental disability. And some defendants dissimulate in both ways. Confirming or ruling out the likelihood of dissimulation is a part of every competence evaluation.

It is helpful to have different names for these two types of dissimulation. Traditionally the dissimulation of symptoms of illness has been called *malingering.* There is no consensus about what to call dissimulation of deficits in competence abilities, but I prefer to use the term *feigning* when referring to efforts to perform poorly in answering questions related to competence abilities.

RESPONSE STYLE AS A SOURCE OF IMPAIRED FUNCTIONING

In recent years, the term *response style* has been offered as a broader concept referring to any pattern of responding by the examinee that produces error if one takes their performance at face value as an indicator of their true ability. Malingering and feigning can be seen as response styles. But there are other "patterns of responding" that are not usually called dissimulation, and their relation to legal incompetence is less clear.

For example, a person's low self-esteem might cause the person typically to respond to questions vaguely or with significant ambivalence. This is a "response style" that impairs their performance, but it is not dissimulation (an attempt to appear impaired aimed at personal gain). Similarly, a sullen and oppositional 15-year-old responds to some majority of the examiner's questions about trial-related matters with "I don't know" and "Whatever." Nothing in the other data for the evaluation suggests dissimulation. Are these cases in which the individual might be found incompetent?

They might be, if the conditions themselves (low self-esteem; oppositional attitude) are strongly related to one of the three conditions that we reviewed as potential reasons for incompetence—in the first case a diagnosis of Major Depression, and in the second a relation to developmental immaturity. But if they appear to be manifestations of enduring personality traits, the answer is less clear and may depend on local judicial practices.

In summary, the *Causal objective* requires that the examiner acquire information that will do three things:

- Verify the nature of any symptoms of mental disorder, presence of developmental disability, or existence of developmental immaturity
- Verify the presence or absence of any of the other three "non-qualifying" conditions
- Attempt to define the possible relation between any of the conditions and any deficits in competency abilities that have been observed

The last task is sometimes referred to as developing evidence for "links" or the "nexus" between deficits and underlying conditions that may be causing them. What best accounts for the deficits in the defendant's competence abilities? And more specifically, *how* does it account for them? For example, the defendant may have delusions, and the defendant may be expressing some illogical things about the prosecutor. But that does not mean that the delusions are "causing" the illogical beliefs about the prosecutor. In what way does the actual content of the defendant's delusion *bear a direct relation to* his or her misconceptions about the prosecutor? Such inferences will be discussed further in Chapter 5.

THE INTERACTIVE OBJECTIVE

The evaluation should provide information that suggests the degree of significance of the defendant's functional deficits in light of specific demands of the defendant's case.

The *Interactive objective* examines the defendant's abilities in relation to the demands of the case. Appendix C offers a list of ways in which trial circumstances (demands) can vary across cases. Examples include "probable length of the trial" and "complexity and multiplicity of charges." The degree of a defendant's functional deficits may be more or less important in different case circumstances. Examiners assist the court when they can describe whether the strengths and weaknesses in a defendant's abilities are a "match" or "mismatch" regarding the demands of this defendant's own case. This objective is called "interactive" because it considers the defendant's abilities and the trial demands in interaction.

This objective may sound complex at first, but it is actually quite simple. Not being able to calculate arithmetic fractions is not, in itself, a deficit. It is a deficit for purposes of reducing or increasing the amounts of ingredients described in recipes when one faces more or fewer guests. But it is not a deficit for purposes of playing the violin. Deficits are not simply things a person cannot do. From an interactive perspective, they are things that impair functioning in some specific context.

For example, imagine a 16-year-old youth who has been transferred to criminal court for trial as an adult on a serious crime. The youth is now being evaluated for competence to stand trial. The youth has long had a diagnosis of ADHD with serious difficulties maintaining attention. One of the functional abilities included in the question of competence to stand trial is the defendant's ability to follow the proceedings of the trial. The youth is able to maintain fairly good attention for a short period of time—10 to 15 minutes—but cannot maintain it longer than that. The importance of this deficit for considering competence, therefore, will depend on whether the youth is likely to have to endure prolonged trial sessions. The examiner provides the information about attention span and notes that this will be a problem only if the trial sessions are of their usual length. In doing this, the examiner provides the court the necessary information allowing the court to weigh the significance of the deficits in light of the court's expectations about the length of the defendant's future trial.

The Interactive objective recognizes that the law does not associate any specific degree of ability with legal competence. The "sufficient" and "reasonable" levels of ability mentioned in the *Dusky* definition are defined no more precisely, partly because they will vary from case to case. Thus it is possible for two defendants to have identical degrees of deficit on the same competence abilities, yet for one defendant to be declared incompetent and the other competent. Similarly, a defendant's degree of deficit may result in a finding of competence if the defendant is facing one particular set of trial circumstances but a finding of incompetent in another set of trial circumstances.

For example, imagine that a defendant is totally amnestic for the period of time during which he is said to have engaged in the criminal act with which he is charged. He cannot tell his lawyer his side of the story regarding the events during the critical days in question. The attorney, therefore, is without the defendant's own recollection to build a defense. Does the defendant have "insufficient present ability" to consult with his lawyer? The courts say, "It depends." (For example, *Wilson v. U.S*, 1968.) Is this a case in which the prosecutor's facts can only be rebutted by the defendant's recollection of the events? Or is it a case in which ten unrelated people will testify that they saw the defendant in a town 500 miles away from the crime scene all of the day in question? In the latter case, the defendant's amnestic deficit may be of little significance at all for the fairness of the trial, and therefore it may offer little reason for a judicial conclusion of incompetence.

The examiner's fulfillment of the Interactive objective does not require the examiner to anticipate precisely what the defendant's trial demands will be. The way the examiner contributes to this balancing of the defendant's deficits against trial demands is *simply to identify the connection between the defendant's incapacities and potential trial demands.* For example, if the defendant has a paranoid (psychotic) delusion that causes him to distrust women, and if the defendant's attorney is a woman, the examiner may simply point out that the defendant's paranoid delusion is less likely to influence his ability to assist counsel if the attorney is a male. Similarly, in our first example of the boy with ADHD, the examiner has no way of knowing how long the trial sessions will be. But the examiner can inform the court that the youth would be able to tolerate sessions only up to 10 to 20 minutes. This provides the court better information than merely stating that the youth has a "serious attention deficit that may interfere with his ability to follow the trial." It is the court, of course, that will determine whether this warrants a finding of competence or incompetence.

THE CONCLUSORY OBJECTIVE

The examiner may provide an opinion concerning whether the defendant is competent or incompetent to stand trial.

The *Conclusory objective* answers the ultimate legal question in competence cases: Are the defendant's deficits sufficiently serious that they threaten the fairness of putting the defendant to trial? When a judge declares competence or incompetence to stand trial, this is the question the judge is answering.

Notice the word "may" in the above definition of the Conclusory objective. Most state laws permit forensic mental health examiners to offer an opinion on the answer to this question in competence cases. Federal law does as well (although not for opinions on criminal responsibility). The court is not required to follow the examiner's opinion, of course. But many courts routinely ask that examiners conclude their competence report with an opinion of competence or incompetence to stand trial.

You may encounter some judges, however, who do not want the forensic examiner's opinion about this "ultimate legal question" of competence. The opinions they want are about the other objectives: functional abilities, causes for deficits, interactive implications of the deficits, and (as described later) prospects for remediation. They believe that the conclusion about whether the defendant is or is not competent is an opinion about whether the facts of the case meet the legal definition, which they believe is properly answered by the trier of fact, not a witness in the case.

When courts do not clearly specify their preference about this, what guidance has our field provided for best practice? There has been controversy for many years among forensic clinicians about the appropriateness of forensic examiners offering conclusory opinions on legal competence. Some surveys (e.g., Borum & Grisso, 1996) have found that most seasoned forensic mental health examiners believe that it is acceptable to do so. A significant minority, however, claimed that it was inappropriate. The *Specialty Guidelines for Forensic Psychology* (American Psychology-Law Society and American Academy of Forensic Psychology, 2011) neither encourages nor prohibits it but requires that forensic examiners understand the issue and be able to explain whatever approach they take in practice.

Several points are made by those who believe that examiners should not offer a conclusory opinion on competence to stand trial:

- It is unnecessary, because it offers the court no new information for its consideration. "Competence to stand trial" is not a clinical condition.
- The conclusion by definition requires a decision about whether the defendant's deficits are sufficient to threaten the fairness of the trial. Nothing in clinical data or theory informs one's opinion of "how much incapacity is enough to create unfairness or injustice." It is a legal and moral question.
- Some courts themselves do not understand this distinction and believe that forensic clinicians have specialized knowledge to discern competence vs. incompetence. Offering a conclusory opinion furthers this misunderstanding and encourages judges to presume that they should agree with the examiner.

Those forensic experts who are comfortable with offering conclusory opinions offer the following points to consider:

- Offering an opinion assists the court in considering the weight of the data to support the opinion.
- It does no harm, in that courts understand that this is only a forensic expert's opinion and has no authority to conclude the matter.

- Reluctance to offer a conclusory opinion can actually confuse the issue, especially if the examiner seems to be implying a conclusion without being willing to announce it.

THE DISPOSITIONAL OBJECTIVE

"Disposition" refers to court orders regarding what will be done as a result of a finding of incompetence. *In cases in which the court finds the defendant incompetent, the evaluation should provide information that the court can use to decide on matters of treatment or other remediation to try to reduce deficits related to incompetence to stand trial.*

The *Dispositional objective* is to address questions about remediation (as noted in Chapter 1, often called "restoration of competence"). To assist the court regarding a disposition of an incompetence case, examiners should collect data and provide relevant information to address the following questions:

- Are the defendant's deficits in functional abilities remediable?
- If remediable, what treatment would be required?
- Within what general length of time would a desired effect be expected?
- Where can this treatment best be accomplished?
- What conditions of restriction (e.g., secure programming) might be required?

As noted in Chapter 1, the purpose for providing this information is not to describe treatment that would be required to restore the individual to be able to function in the community. The goal is modification of the defendant's condition sufficiently to remediate the deficits in competence to stand trial abilities. Sometimes the dispositional recommendation is the same for either of those goals. But often individuals who are restored to competence still have symptoms that would make their general adaptation to community life difficult. Subsequent chapters will describe ways to address these questions raised about remediation.

A COMMENT ON IRRELEVANT OBJECTIVES

Reviewing these objectives for competence to stand trial evaluations, it is evident that general clinical evaluations will never serve the courts' purposes adequately in competence cases. The evaluations that are valuable in clinical settings to describe patients' broad capacities and disabilities and to formulate treatment plans would lack data that are needed to address each of the five objectives of competence evaluations.

Moreover, general clinical evaluations would contain data that are *not* relevant for purposes of addressing the competence evaluation objectives. *One of the primary guiding principles of forensic evaluations is that they should only contain information that is relevant for the legal question.* Similarly, evaluations conducted for the courts are not "all-purpose" forensic evaluations. They should address only the legal question that the court asks.

Therefore, competence evaluations and reports rarely say anything about a defendant's ability to know right from wrong (relevant to criminal responsibility) or risk of future recidivism or violence. There is nothing in the competence question that requires (or allows) any comment on the causes of a defendant's past criminal behavior in a competence to stand trial evaluation.

OBJECTIVES FOR TYPES OF COMPETENCE TO STAND TRIAL EVALUATIONS

There are several different contexts in which competence evaluations are performed. Everything discussed in this chapter applies to competence evaluations of all kinds. But they may place greater or lesser emphasis on certain objectives.

Some jurisdictions employ *brief or screening competence evaluations.* Competence screening evaluations typically are abbreviated in their data collection, often relying on a single, brief interview and little or no other data. The use of competence screening evaluations has arisen in some jurisdictions to avoid, where possible, the use of unnecessary time and resources and not to prolong the adjudication process for the defendant. If screening suggests that the defendant is clearly competent, no further evaluation may be needed. But if there remains even a small likelihood of incompetence, the examiner suggests to the court a full competence evaluation. Screening is focused only on the Functional and Causal objectives. Moreover, the examiner does not intend to provide a complete answer to these objectives, but merely enough to determine whether there is any doubt about the defendant's competence abilities or mental condition.

The second type of competence evaluations are *full competence evaluations.* These will be found in every jurisdiction. All five of the objectives, of course, are relevant for these evaluations.

The third type is *competence restoration evaluations.* These are performed with defendants who were found incompetent to stand trial and have been provided treatment or other interventions to remediate their competence deficits. Their purpose is to determine whether the deficits that were responsible for the defendant's incompetence have been reduced or whether further treatment is needed—and if so, whether it is likely to improve the defendant's abilities. Generally these are much like full competence evaluations, but they have the benefit of beginning with the baseline information that the defendant's original evaluation provides. All five of the evaluation objectives are relevant.

We are now ready to proceed to a description of methods for competence to stand trial evaluations. Selection of methods follows closely the five objectives reviewed in this chapter.

Chapter 3

SELECTING METHODS

This chapter describes specific assessment methods with which the examiner can pursue each of the objectives outlined in Chapter 2. Do not expect to be offered a "standard battery" of methods to use in all competence to stand trial assessments. As in any other clinical evaluation, the methods used must vary somewhat from case to case, based on basic differences among defendants and the questions that their cases raise. The examiner must use clinical judgment when selecting methods for a particular case.

Method selection should be guided by values that are common to clinical assessment generally. One of those values is the reduction of potential sources of error in data collection and interpretation.

A primary requirement for reducing error is to employ *standardized* methods whenever possible. A data collection method is "standardized" when its procedure is sufficiently clear to allow various examiners to collect their data in the same way. For example, the method may standardize the questions and the sequence in which they are asked, the response format, ways of evaluating the quality of the examinee's responses, and other matters of procedure. This also means that a single examiner will be able to use the method to collect data in the same way across cases or in the same case at different times (e.g., to assess change in competence abilities as a consequence of remediation).

Another quality to consider is the degree to which research has demonstrated the *reliability and validity* of the method's results. Psychometric methods with fixed items and relatively objective scoring systems tend to fare better in reliability studies than do less structured methods. This does not mean, of course, that the examiner's methods should be limited to psychometric tests. Tests are important for many reasons, but often they do not provide the breadth, depth, or flexibility needed by the examiner to explore certain types of information related to competence that might be relatively unique to an individual case.

Research with some assessment methods has demonstrated that their results are actually related to behaviors and abilities that are relevant for legal questions. These results contribute to the method's validity—the evidence that it measures what it claims to measure. For example, some tools designed to assess defendants' competence abilities have been shown to produce substantially lower scores on average for persons who have been found incompetent by courts. When you use these methods, it allows you to testify with greater confidence about the meaning of the evaluation for the legal issue.

One of the best hedges against error and unreliability is to test your interpretations by requiring that they be supported by *multiple sources of data*. This reminds us that often we may want to use more than one method to assess competence abilities or clinical symptoms. The two methods may be a test and an interview, two tests, or behavior observed in an interview and the report of a third party's observation outside the evaluation setting. The main benefit of this practice is that it reduces "method error"—the possibility that the defendant's behavior seen in any one method may be more or less specific only to that method at that point in time. Further, the logic of multiple data sources is easily understood by courts and juries. The need for multiple sources of data is prominently featured in all published guidelines for forensic evaluations, including competence evaluations.

DATA FOR THE FUNCTIONAL OBJECTIVE

Chapter 2 pointed out that the Functional objective requires the assessment of defendants' abilities that are relevant specifically for the question of competence to stand trial. Further, we noted that it is best to assess these matters directly, rather than to make inferences about them from assessments of more general intellectual and personality characteristics.

SEMISTRUCTURED INTERVIEWS AND STANDARDIZED APPROACHES

Every competence evaluation must employ a semistructured interview that focuses specifically on defendants' competence abilities and deficits.

The interview must aim to discover those things that the defendant understands, believes, and can do that are relevant for participating in a defense. Most forensic clinicians have developed their own sets of questions for these interviews or have adopted a set of questions from their mentors. Appendix C offers a variety of ways to classify and organize the abilities to be assessed, which provides some structure around which to build competence interview questions.

In recent years, practice standards have encouraged augmenting the competence interview with standardized competence assessment tools to assess legally relevant abilities and deficits. The reasons for this are associated with the previous discussion about standardization. This allows for reduction in sources of error as well as support for one's interpretations based on research that used the standardized and structured methods. Later in this section we will review some of these tools.

However, using one of these tools does not remove the necessity for a more individualized competence abilities interview. This is recognized and explicitly acknowledged in the manuals of most of the tools described later. There are two reasons for this. First, using structured approaches alone increases the risk of missing individualized features, because their standardization sometimes inhibits exploration of idiosyncratic characteristics. Second, no competence assessment tool assesses all of the functional abilities that are relevant for the legal concept of competence to stand trial. For example, the instruments reviewed later vary in the range of things that they ask about factual Understanding, in the manner in which they explore Appreciation, and in the degree to which they explore difficulties in Reasoning that may influence decision making.

Many examiners, therefore, use a standardized competence assessment tool, then engage in further, nonstandardized interviewing about the competence abilities. The latter can aim to explore any types of relevant competence abilities that the tool does not assess. It can also explore deficits that may have arisen in the standardized competence tool but that were especially idiosyncratic, odd, or puzzling in a way that suggests the need for more detailed or creative inquiry.

The following discussion describes some of the standardized methods for assessing competence abilities and deficits. Only the more recent and most frequently used methods are described here. Descriptions of the full range of methods can be found in various sources (Grisso, 2003; Melton et al., 2007; Zapf & Roesch, 2009), which also provide detailed information about the empirical foundation for these tools (their reliability and validity).

In addition, Grisso and colleagues have reviewed 25 years of research on competence to stand trial instruments at 5-year intervals in the journal *Behavioral Sciences and the Law* (Grisso, 1992, for research publications during 1986-1990; Cooper & Grisso, 1997, for 1991-1995; Mumley, Grisso, & Tillbrook, 2003, for 1996-2000; and Fogel et al., 2013, for 2001-2010).

Note that Appendix D of this book provides information for obtaining manuals and testing materials for the instruments described in this section.

Zapf and Roesch (2009) developed a handy way to classify these methods. They include: (a) ideographic methods, (b) nomothetic methods, and (c) methods for special populations. We add to this a fourth source of information about competence abilities that involves neither tools nor standardization but has substantial importance: (d) archival and observational data.

IDIOGRAPHIC STANDARDIZED METHODS

Idiographic methods typically are not psychometric. They favor individualized descriptions of defendants' competence abilities and deficits. Their formats bear resemblance to psychological tools that employ "structured professional judgment" (SPJ). SPJ tools offer structure for directing an examiner's inquiry so that it gets data that is conceptually relevant for the objective. But typically SPJ tools do not use standardized or highly structured interview questions. They may require ratings of each type of data, but the ratings are not processed mathematically, yield no total scores, and offer no norms with which to compare examinees. Actuarial benefits are sacrificed in favor of the ability to get rich, individualized information in a structured format.

The Competency Assessment Instrument (CAI)

The CAI was among the first structured tools to guide competence abilities interviews. It was developed in the early 1970s by A. Louis McGarry and his colleagues in a large-scale research project. The manual for the CAI was in a government monograph reporting the results of McGarry's research project. It is long out of print and has no distributor. It may be obtained from some university libraries.

The CAI guided the interviewer to ask questions that would elicit information from a defendant related to 13 "functions" (or competency abilities) developed in that project. These "functions," listed in Appendix C, continue to be a guide for many competence examiners today. They structure the type of information the examiner should elicit, and they suggest certain types of questions for an interview. But the CAI offers no actual standardized set of interview questions. It does instruct the examiner to rate information gained about each of the 13 functions (on a 0-5 scale). But it offers no objective definitions for assigning ratings and does not produce an overall score. Thus it has no norms.

The CAI's primary value has been as a method to structure examiners' interview questions, and it can do this quite well in light of the high degree of face validity of the 13 competency functions. The primary weakness of the method is that one cannot claim any empirical validity for one's results as an indicator of defendants' competence abilities.

Fitness Interview Test-Revised (FIT-R)

The FIT was originally developed in 1984 and then revised and adapted as the FIT-R for use in the U.S. in 2006 by Roesch, Zapf, and Eaves. ("Competence to stand trial" is called "fitness" in Canada.) The FIT-R has items that parallel the standard for competence established in Canada and the federal U.S. standard. The items in the tool's semi-structured interview format are conceptually clustered in three areas:

- Ability to understand the nature or object of the proceedings, or factual knowledge of criminal procedure
- Ability to understand the possible consequences of the proceedings, or the appreciation of personal involvement in the importance of the proceedings
- Ability to communicate with counsel, or to participate in the defense

Each item is rated (0-2), but the ratings contribute to neither summaries for the above three scales nor to an overall competence score. Considerable research has demonstrated that the items can be rated reliably and that it produces scores that are generally consistent with other indices of trial competence or incompetence. The tool is especially designed to describe defendants' competence in an "ideographic" fashion: that is, with less emphasis on normative comparisons and more on an individualized description of the defendant's capacities.

NOMOTHETIC STANDARDIZED METHODS

Methods with a nomothetic objective produce scores or ratings for each item, and the scores are combined to produce summary scores on conceptual scales. This allows the development of norms to which an individual examinee can be compared, suggesting the degree of abilities or deficits in relation to comparison samples. Nomothetic methods require greater standardization of items or interview questions. This reduces the examiner's ability to explore the more individualized ways in which an examinee might manifest deficits in competence abilities. In effect, these tools sacrifice some of the advantages of ideographic methods in favor of the advantages of norms and of data that are most amenable to use in research studies of the tool's validity.

MacArthur Competence Assessment Tool - Criminal Adjudication (MacCAT-CA)

The MacCAT-CA evolved out of an extensive research project during the 1990s by the MacArthur Research Network on Mental Health and Law. The project developed an array of research measures designed to test hypotheses about the relation between mental illness and defendants' trial competence. Subsequently the group borrowed on the research measures to create a tool, the MacCAT-CA, that was feasible for routine clinical use in competence to stand trial evaluations. Additional research with the MacCAT-CA established its initial reliability and validity (Poythress et al., 1999).

The MacCAT-CA was published by Psychological Assessment Resources, Inc., in 1999. It consists of a highly structured interview (questions are asked verbatim as they appear in the manual), employing 22 items that require about 35 to 45 minutes to administer. The interview employs a hypothetical crime situation involving two men, with questions designed to assess defendants' capacities in three areas:

- *understanding* the roles of trial participants, elements of an offense, consequences of conviction, and pleading
- *reasoning* about such matters as possible mitigating factors and implications of choices that the defendant may have to make
- realistic *appreciation* of the likelihood of various possible outcomes and trial events

Administration of the interview questions must follow the standard sequence, and very specific and objective criteria are provided for scoring. The process yields a score for each of the above three areas with no composite "competence" score. The scores can be compared to those of groups of individuals who were found competent or incompetent to stand trial.

One of the helpful features of the MacCAT-CA is its procedure that allows one to examine whether defendants can "learn" things that they do not currently understand about trials. On several items, if the defendant does not provide an adequate answer, the examiner uses a standardized procedure for "teaching" the defendant the relevant information or concept. Then the defendant is retested on that item to determine whether the defendant has the capacity to grasp the information.

Evaluation of Competency to Stand Trial-Revised (ECST-R)

The ECST-R was developed by Rogers, Tillbrook and Sewell and published in 2004. It includes an interview guided by 18 semistructured and structured items, requiring about 30 to 40 minutes. The items allow for somewhat more exploration than in the MacCAT-CA. The questions focus on the defendant's own potential legal circumstances, not a hypothetical situation as in the MacCAT-CA. Objective anchors are offered to score the information gained from each of these items. The item scores contribute to scores on four scales:

- Factual understanding of courtroom proceedings
- Rational Understanding of the courtroom proceedings
- Consult with counsel
- Overall rational ability (raw scores for the two scales immediately above)

The scores on these scales do not lead to an overall "competence score," and the tool does not offer "cut-off scores" to determine whether a defendant is competent or incompetent on any of the scales. Scores can be compared to those of groups of individuals who were found competent or incompetent to stand trial.

A feature that distinguishes the ECST-R from all other competence to stand trial assessment tools is its inclusion of items that contribute to five response-style scales. These assist in screening for defendants who might be feigning incompetence. "Screening" means that the tool does not try to predict feigning, but seeks to identify defendants who warrant additional scrutiny with more specialized methods.

Differences Between the MacCAT-CA and the ECST-R

These two tools have substantial differences in their formats. When considering which of them one prefers, the following differences should be recognized:

- The MacCAT-CA uses a hypothetical case to discuss what the defendant understands or can reason about, while the ECST-R interview is based on the defendant's own situation.
- The ECST-R offers a semistructured approach to the questions that defendant is asked, while the MacCAT-CA requires close adherence to the specific wording of each item.
- The scoring criteria for the MacCAT-CA are somewhat more clear (and rigid) than those in the ECST-R.
- The ECST-R provides a method for raising the question of dissimulation of incompetence, a feature not found in the MacCAT-CA.

STANDARDIZED METHODS FOR SPECIAL POPULATIONS

Among competence ability assessment tools that have been developed for special populations, two are encountered most frequently. One is for use with persons with developmental disabilities and the other with children and adolescents.

Competence Assessment for Standing Trial for Defendants with Mental Retardation (CAST-MR)

The CAST-MR was developed by Everington and Luckasson in the early 1990s to use in assessing competence of defendants with developmental disabilities (mental retardation). It uses a highly structured format of 50 interview questions divided into three sections. Two of these sections—Basic Legal Concepts, and Skills to Assist Defense—use a multiple-choice format for which the examinee chooses the "best" answer. The third section—Understanding Case Events—uses open-ended questions that are scored to identify the individual's ability to communicate information about the individual's case in an accurate manner.

The features of the CAST-MR were chosen specifically because they address problems that examiners encounter in evaluating persons with developmental disabilities. Developmental disabilities often create special problems in the ability to communicate with counsel, the focus of the third section. The CAST-MR's unusual use of multiple-choice items was designed because persons with developmental disabilities often have difficulties with verbal expression. The use of open-ended interview items, the format of choice in other competence tools, runs the risk that such defendants may actually understand the necessary information but are unable to express it. A multiple-choice format reduces the need for translating what one knows into words to express one's thoughts.

Juvenile Adjudicative Competence Interview (JACI)

The JACI currently is the only tool designed specifically to assist in competence to stand trial evaluations of juveniles. It was devised by Grisso in 2005 as part of a MacArthur Foundation project that included research on adolescents' competence abilities (Grisso et al., 2003) and the development of standards and methods for performing competence to stand trial evaluations in juvenile cases.

The JACI is a semistructured interview that includes 42 interview questions across 13 areas of inquiry (such as "Possible Pleas," "Assisting the Attorney," and "Reasoning and Decision Making"). Each area of inquiry includes one or two "Understanding" items and one or two "Appreciation" items. One section uses a detailed hypothetical offer of a plea agreement to assess youths' capacities to think about short-range and longer-range consequences. Each item has a description of what is being assessed, but no ratings or scores are given. The tool is designed simply to provide structure for the interview.

The items, though, are different from other competence tools in two ways that are driven by special problems in assessing adolescents' competence. First, many adolescents appear to have adequate factual understanding, yet they have concrete misperceptions of legal concepts that impair their ability to apply what they understand. For example, even though they might understand what it means to plead not guilty, it is more common for adolescents than for adults to believe that defendants can plead not guilty only if they did not commit the alleged offense. They "understand" but they have concrete misperceptions about how things work. The JACI format decreases the likelihood that the examiner will miss these underlying difficulties often associated with adolescents' developmentally less-mature appreciation.

Second, many of the items provide the youth with points of comparison that use young people's familiarity with similar or dissimilar concepts in everyday life. For example, "Imagine your school principal calls you in to tell you that you did something wrong. How is that the same or different from a trial in court?" Finally, some items use a "teaching" process when the youth does not understand some component of the trial process, providing for a reassessment on those items at the end of the interview (to examine the young person's retention of what was taught). This information may be useful in making estimates about remediation.

A Note on Use of "Adult" Competence Tools with Adolescents

Only very limited information has been available on the use of the MacCAT-CA and ECST-R with adolescents (Fogel et al., 2013; Mumley et al., 2003). This does not mean that they cannot be used. But if examiners are considering their use with adolescents, there are several matters to keep in mind.

First, certain types of content that are included in the MacCAT-CA and ECST-R may not be ideal for circumstances of trials in juvenile court. Examining youths' knowledge of the purpose and role of juries, for example, is irrelevant for juvenile court hearings in all but a few states. Second, certain types of content that are especially important for assessing adolescents are not represented in most instruments. For example, some research suggests that youths on average are immature (compared to adults) in their appraisal of consequences when weighing their choices in legal circumstances. The adult tools are not structured to explore these matters specifically. Finally, to date there are no norms for adolescents on the MacCAT-CA or ECST-R.

Nevertheless, a research effort by the MacArthur Foundation (Grisso et al., 2003) demonstrated that the MacCAT-CA can be used with adolescents, with certain cautions. At least with the MacCAT-CA's Understanding and Reasoning scales, the MacCAT-CA can be used to compare an adolescent's performance to that of adults, which might be helpful in cases involving juveniles who are being tried in adult criminal court. But in cases involving juvenile court hearings, currently there is no empirical information with which to compare adolescents to adolescent samples on the MacCAT-CA or the ECST-R.

ARCHIVAL AND OBSERVATIONAL DATA

Some of the most important information related to the Functional objective comes from examination of defendants' files, third-party sources, and observations in nonstandardized situations.

Mental Health Files

Clinical files sometimes contain reports of competence evaluations performed in prior adjudications or comments regarding the defendant's behaviors in past trials. These data cannot be considered evidence of the defendant's current competence abilities, but they may prepare the examiner to look into issues that would not otherwise have been anticipated.

Attorneys and Judges

Frequently it is helpful to learn from judges and attorneys what behaviors of the defendant caused them to raise the question of incompetence. This helps to define the "referral question" and can alert you to specific areas of functioning that may need special scrutiny. For example, an attorney might report that in consultation, the defendant seemed "intelligent enough" but told a very confused story about events on the night of the offense that the attorney could not understand. This will alert you to pay especially close attention to the defendant's capacity to provide counsel with an intelligible account of events (from the defendant's perspective) related to the charges, without which the attorney may be significantly hampered in developing a defense.

Observing Attorney-Client Interactions

One way to assess defendants' abilities to relate to an attorney is by observing them in actual interaction with their attorneys. This opportunity occasionally arises naturally as a result of the attorney's presence at the examination session, while in other instances examiners have asked attorneys to attend in order to allow the examiner to observe the client-attorney interaction.

The examiner who employs this method will have to improvise, because forensic assessment literature offers no description of it. One can generalize from clinical practice. For example, many clinicians who have performed family assessments are familiar with the technique of giving families a task to perform or a problem to solve together, then observing their behaviors and interactions as they carry out the assignment. Similarly, forensic examiners might wish to develop their own set of tasks appropriate for client-attorney discussion, during which the examiner can observe the defendant's manner of handling the tasks in collaboration with the attorney.

DATA FOR THE CAUSAL OBJECTIVE

The Causal objective requires data that will provide possible explanations for deficits observed during the assessment of the defendant's competence abilities. Across pretrial competence cases, these explanations may include not only many psychological and neurological disorders, but also situational (e.g., fatigue) and motivational (e.g., malingering) explanations.

ARCHIVAL AND THIRD-PARTY OBSERVATIONAL DATA

Part of meeting the Causal objective involves obtaining the same types of archival and third-party sources of information that clinicians typically obtain for general clinical evaluations. Records of past mental health contacts may provide information addressing questions of diagnosis and chronicity, as well as treatment potential. Criminal justice records and the observations of jail or psychiatric staff where the defendant currently is being held often provide observations of symptomatic behavior. These data may substantiate or challenge the examiner's own diagnostic impressions based on more direct observation.

PSYCHOPATHOLOGY: MENTAL STATUS INTERVIEW METHODS AND TESTS

Experienced mental health professionals will be familiar with the range of methods for addressing questions of psychiatric diagnosis. Generally they include interview methods and psychological tests.

Mental Status Exams

Many clinicians include a formal mental status exam at some point in their interview process. Mental status exams employ a minimum number of standardized questions to elicit information about basic mental functions (e.g., orientation, memory, fund of information attention). Performance often reveals deficits that lead to hypotheses about mental disorders or intellectual disabilities.

In addition, efficiency and accountability in courtroom testimony can be enhanced by adopting a standardized interview designed to assist in differential diagnosis of disorders. Quite a number of such methods are now available, including structured mental status examinations and structured diagnostic interview tools like the Diagnostic Interview Schedule and the Schedule for Affective Disorder and Schizophrenia. Rogers (2001) has provided an excellent review of the full range of structured diagnostic interview methods as well as mental status examinations.

General Clinical Interview

The open-ended clinical interview in competence evaluations typically focuses on the defendant's history, social adaptation, and functioning in everyday life. Usually the history taking does not need to be as extensive as it might be in many general clinical examinations. Its main purpose is narrower: to rule out or substantiate underlying psychological conditions that might explain deficits in competence abilities, rather than developing a full "working model" of the defendant's personality. But various aspects of the defendant's history often play a role in the examiner's reasoning about causes of the defendant's current deficits. Often the history focuses on education, social networks and interpersonal relations, employment history and functioning, and history of involvements with the criminal or juvenile justice system.

Psychological Tests for Psychopathology

Many competence evaluations include objective tests assessing psychopathology (e.g., the *Minnesota Multiphasic Personality Inventory-2*, Butcher et al., 1989; *the Child Behavior Checklist*, Achenbach & Rescorla, 2001) and devices for characterizing symptom severity (e.g., *Brief Psychiatric Rating Scale*, Overall & Gorham, 1962). These provide results to augment and cross-check information from the interview methods noted above. There is no "best" measure of psychopathology for competence evaluations. Typically they are selected at the discretion of the examiner, on the basis of their ability to test the examiners' hypotheses in that particular case.

INTELLECTUAL FUNCTIONING (DEVELOPMENTAL DISABILITY)

Most mental health professionals can make rough judgments about a person's general level of intellectual functioning on the basis of a clinical interview. But few clinicians can demonstrate the reliability of their IQ estimates, and attorneys who do not agree with your estimate may ask you to demonstrate why the court should trust your "guess." If developmental disability is to be ruled out, typically this should involve the use of psychometric instruments for evaluating intellectual functioning—that is, standardized intelligence tests for adults or for children.

An IQ score is not the only important information that intelligence tests provide for competence evaluations. A defendant's performance on the various subscales of the WAIS-IV sometimes reveals how the defendant's psychopathology interferes with cognitive processes involving recall of distant and immediate events, logic in decision making, and verbal comprehension. When symptoms interfere with these cognitive functions, this may have implications for the defendant's ability to deal cognitively with future trial events. Therefore, WAIS-IV results often are helpful to establish a link between psychopathology and the trial-relevant abilities about which the law is concerned.

Remember that if a diagnosis of developmental disability must be established, an intelligence test is not enough. It also requires an assessment of the individual's adaptive functioning in a broader sphere of activities in daily life. Some examiners use structured tools for this as well: for example, the *Independent Living Scale* (Loeb, 1996) or the *Vineland Adaptive Behavior Scales* (Sparrow, Cicchetti, & Balla, 2005).

ORGANIC MENTAL DISORDERS

Neurological examination may be needed when there is initial reason to suspect that deficits one has observed in a defendant's competence abilities may be due to brain trauma or disease. For example, defendants sometimes claim amnesia due to head injuries related to fights and accidents occurring near the time of their arrest. This may require an examination to determine whether actual neurological damage was sustained. Neuropsychological tests often can determine cognitive functions that have been impaired by brain disorder. Complex cases might require the assistance of a specialized forensic neuropsychologist.

DEVELOPMENTAL IMMATURITY

Children or adolescents may perform poorly with regard to functional competence abilities for reasons other than mental illness or developmental disability. Especially if they are 14 or younger, their capacities for understanding or appreciating various aspects of trials and their outcomes may be inferior to those of most adults simply because of their developmental immaturity. Considerable evidence indicates that they are less likely to have the capacities of adults for judgment in making decisions that defendants are expected to make (Grisso et al., 2003). Assessing cognitive and emotional maturity, therefore, is an important part of competence evaluations of juveniles.

Intelligence tests and social maturity scales sometimes can identify youths whose cognitive or social capacities are developmentally delayed in relation to their peers. What are needed, however, are measures that more specifically assess developmental status in certain capacities that influence decision making (e.g., capacity for time perspective, ability to use abstractions in problem solving or decision making, and realistic perceptions of risks). Some instruments of this type do exist in the research literature, but they have not been sufficiently developed for routine clinical forensic use. Recommendations for assessing cognitive and psychosocial immaturity in clinical interviews are provided in a book developed as part of a MacArthur Research Network project, called *Evaluating Juveniles' Adjudicative Competence: A Guide for Clinical Practice* (Grisso, 2005).

DISSIMULATION

Recall from Chapter 2 that malingering refers to dissimulation of symptoms, while feigning is the term we are using for dissimulating deficits in competence abilities. Dissimulation must be considered as a possible cause in *every* case in which a defendant shows deficits in competence abilities or displays symptoms of mental illness or developmental disability. This is not because it is always a strong rival hypothesis in such cases, but because you must always be able to respond to the reasonable question by the attorney who needs to challenge your opinion: "Doctor, how do you know the defendant wasn't malingering?"

Chapter 5 will explain that attempts to detect dissimulation of deficits and disorders rely substantially on one's ability to spot inconsistencies and illogical patterns in the defendant's presentation of pathological signs (Rogers, 2012). This almost always requires obtaining diagnostic information from several sources, since it is more difficult for defendants to present a consistent picture across different environmental settings (e.g., the ward and the clinical interview) or across tests with different formats. Obtaining archival information and observation from outside the evaluation setting, as well as multiple measures of psychopathology, provides the best way to detect inconsistencies related to malingering.

A number of assessment tools are available for identifying defendants who might be malingering mental disorders or feigning deficits in competence abilities. They range from "validity" scales on general tests for psychopathology (e.g., the MMPI-2) to highly specialized instruments such as the *Structured Interview of Reported Symptoms-2* (SIRS-2; Rogers, Sewell, & Gillard, 2010) and the *Validity Indicator Profile* (VIP; Frederick, 1997). Tests for malingering of specific symptoms are also available, such as the *Test of Memory Malingering* (TOMM; Tombaugh, 1996) and the *Structured Inventory of Malingered Symptomatology* (SIMS; Widows & Smith, 2005). In addition, as noted earlier, the *Evaluation of Competency to Stand Trial-Revised* (ECST-R) has a set of scales that are specifically designed to assess dissimulation within the context of the competence evaluation.

Regarding adolescents' dissimulation, McCann (1998) has provided a careful overview of methods and issues associated with assessment of malingering among adolescents. The SIRS also has been used with adolescent offenders (Rogers, Hinds & Sewell, 1996).

DATA FOR THE INTERACTIVE OBJECTIVE

Chapter 2 explained that the examiner's evaluation can be made more relevant for the court if the defendant's deficits in competence abilities can be compared to the demands of specific trial circumstances in the case. You might anticipate that this requires collecting data about the probable demands of the trial. But typically this is not necessary. Most often it is better not to try to "predict" the demands of the trial, but rather to consider them in a conditional sense (e.g., "If the trial requires X, then the defendant's Y deficit may have considerable impact. . . .").

Nevertheless, sometimes it is helpful to explore the demands. Some of the ways that trial circumstances and demands may vary are listed in Appendix C. Typically the only way to gain information about these possible demands in a specific case is to ask the defendant's attorney to speculate about them. Sometimes this will provide information that rules out the likelihood of certain demands (e.g., the probable need for the defendant to testify), offers a reasonable estimate of the probable length of the trial, or indicates whether it is likely that the defendant may have to make a difficult or complex plea decision. But there are no standardized methods for obtaining information to manage the Interactive objective.

DATA FOR THE CONCLUSORY OBJECTIVE

The Conclusory objective refers to the decision that the results of the evaluation indicate that the defendant is competent or incompetent. One might expect that examiners could use the normative data in the nomothetic tools discussed earlier to arrive at their competence or incompetence decisions. For example, the MacCAT-CA provides scores that can be compared to those of research samples of persons who had been found competent, marginally competent, or incompetent to stand trial. The MacCAT-CA manual, however, strongly warns against using the scores in that way. The examiner's final decision must be based on far more data than are provided by competence assessment tools.

Recall from Chapter 1 that the ultimate question for a conclusion about competence or incompetence is this: "Are the defendant's deficits sufficiently serious that they threaten the fairness of putting the defendant to trial?" We have no data collection methods that represent or measure "fairness."

DATA FOR THE DISPOSITIONAL OBJECTIVE

Chapter 2 explained that the Dispositional objective requires information to determine whether the defendant's deficits in competence abilities are remediable, under what conditions, and requiring what length of time.

Frequently the question of remediability reduces to questions about the predicted effects of appropriate medication, when combined with efforts to "train" the defendant in competence abilities. Questions of where this treatment can be provided, as well as the restrictiveness of the setting, often require consideration of the defendant's psychopathology and degree of self-control, together with knowledge of the conditions of various treatment settings available to the court.

METHODS FOR ASSESSING REMEDIABILITY

Judgments about the type of treatment required for incompetence remediation often rely on diagnostic information obtained with methods described in the section on the Causal objective. In addition, the question of remediability often will hinge on facts obtained from past medical and psychiatric records:

- Information about how the disorder has manifested in this defendant in the past (episodic or continuous; frequent or infrequent)
- The prior course and pattern of disorder (whether there have been periods of stability between episodes, as well as their length)
- Records of past responsiveness or nonresponsiveness to treatment, and the nature of those treatments

Some incompetence cases also call for an assessment of defendants' abilities to profit from instruction aimed at improving their understanding of the trial process. For example, defendants with developmental disability vary in their probable ability to benefit from attempts to teach them about the nature of the trial process and proper roles of its participants. Some may do well, while others may never improve in knowledge even with intensive instruction.

There are few ways to assess this "learning potential" with regarding to specific trial-relevant information. As described earlier in this chapter, the MacCAT-CA offers a structured way to do this, as does the JACI designed for use with adolescent competence cases. For both of these methods, defendants are taught certain concepts that they appear not to comprehend at first, then retested for improvement in their comprehension. Yet neither of these methods has provided empirical evidence that they can estimate learning potential. Moreover, they examine recall after a fairly short period of time, offering insufficient evidence concerning a person's longer-range retention. A more effective approach is to use intellectual or neuropsychological measures of memory and retention of information in general. In cases in which this is an important issue, you should consider consulting a forensic examiner who is specialized in assessments of persons with developmental disability.

ASSESSING TREATMENT OPTIONS

The examiner must know the treatment settings in the community that provide services for remediation of incompetence to stand trial. Typically these will be state-run secure facilities with special units offering such remediation, although in some jurisdictions incompetent defendants are treated on an outpatient basis while they are living in the community outside of jail or any mental health facility. A few jurisdictions also have specialized competence remediation programs for juveniles (as described in Chapter 5).

This chapter has inventoried the more common methods for collecting data related to the five objectives for competence evaluations. Let us turn now to the actual process in which these methods are used.

Chapter 4

COLLECTING THE DATA

This chapter offers recommendations for the process of collecting data for competence to stand trial evaluations. The process begins when the examiner accepts the referral for evaluation. It includes employing a system for documenting the evaluation; preparing the examinee for the evaluation; and performing interviews, testing, and record reviews. It ends when enough data have been collected to move to the formal interpretive stage of the evaluation. In previous chapters we have referred to the person whose competence is being questioned as the "defendant." In this chapter, we will refer to him or her as the "examinee" when the defendant is in that role.

PREPARATION

TAKING THE CASE

Typically there are two circumstances in which examiners receive referrals to perform competence evaluations. They either receive a request from the court, which we will call "court-ordered," or the defendant's attorney may contract independently with the examiner to perform the evaluation, which we will call "private." Reports for court-ordered evaluations typically will be sent to the court, while reports for private evaluations are the property of examinees and their attorneys, who can decide whether or not to introduce the evaluation as evidence in a competence hearing.

Court-ordered evaluations are performed under various referral and financial arrangements (Grisso et al., 1994; Grisso & Quinlan, 2005). In many states they are performed by state or county employees located in public forensic inpatient facilities, in court clinics affiliated with the court itself, or in regional public community mental health centers. Some courts have contracts with independent mental health professionals in the community who perform forensic evaluations at the court's request. Some examiners work in assessment teams, while others work alone. These arrangements are discussed further in Chapter 7.

There are a few circumstances that should give examiners pause to reflect on whether they should accept certain referrals for competence evaluations. These circumstances are all rooted in ethics and guidelines for professional practice.

Need for Special Diagnostic and Clinical Expertise

Initial information may suggest that the case will require specialization with regard to specific assessment methods or diagnostic formulations. For example, when the examiner is not skilled in neuropsychological assessment, initial facts suggesting that the examinee's incapacities may be related to brain trauma might necessitate referral to (or collaboration with) a forensic neuropsychologist.

Of special importance is the age of the examinee. Forensic clinicians who are not trained in child clinical psychiatry or psychology typically should not perform competence to stand trial evaluations of juveniles. Children's and adolescents' mental disorders and developmental disabilities are quite different from those of adults, requiring special expertise in their diagnosis. Psychological testing of children and adolescents requires expert knowledge and skill regarding psychological tests and tools designed specifically for these age groups. In addition, specialized child training typically is required to perform competent interviews of children and adolescents. Evaluating children and adolescents without specialized expertise for this population is contrary to best practices of the mental health professions.

Cultural Competence

Sometimes examinees are immigrants or refugees who have recently come to the U.S. from very different cultural backgrounds. Their grasp of the American legal system may be very poor, and communicating with them and understanding their perspective can be difficult without some knowledge of their culture. The difficulties go beyond matters of language. Even with proper assistance from an interpreter, the meaning and significance of what one learns from examinees with different cultural backgrounds can be misinterpreted or simply missed. This does not mean that examiners must refuse all such cases. But they should do so if they are not willing to spend the time to educate themselves about the cultural background of the examinee.

Dual Roles

Examiners should make every effort to avoid dual role relationships with competence examinees. For example, for inpatient evaluations, a clinician who is responsible for an examinee's treatment typically should not perform the competence evaluation. Treating professionals have different ethical obligations than forensic examiners with regard to confidentiality. Even on small forensic inpatient services, it is often possible for two clinicians to arrange to do forensic evaluations of the other's patients, so that neither is playing both roles for any given forensic patient.

Relations with Attorneys

The examiner should manage the initial contacts with the attorney in a way that does not lead the attorney to believe that the evaluation necessarily will produce information favorable to the defendant's position in the case. Further, in private referrals, fee arrangements should be established clearly before the examiner begins the evaluation, and the fee should not be contingent upon the actual evaluation results or the legal outcome of the case. Examiners who contract with the court to accept court-ordered assessments on an ongoing basis generally will deal with such matters when the contract is negotiated rather than on a case-by-case basis.

CLARIFYING THE QUESTION

Court orders and private requests for forensic evaluations sometimes ask the wrong questions or are not sufficiently specific concerning the legal question to be addressed. For example, court orders for competence evaluations have been known to request an evaluation of the defendant's "ability to know right from wrong," even though this concept is associated with mental state at the time of the crime ("insanity" or "criminal responsibility") rather than competence to stand trial. Therefore, in some court-ordered cases the examiner will have to make an inquiry to the court in order to clarify the referral question. In private cases, this can be done routinely with the lawyer at the first contact.

OBTAINING BACKGROUND INFORMATION

Four general types of information about the case should be obtained before proceeding to interview the examinee. Sometimes the information has not arrived before the time of the first interview and you must simply proceed. But you will do so at some disadvantage, because you will not have basic information to guide your interview questions.

Current Charges

The examiner should obtain basic information about the charges and the nature of the accusations. This is essential. If you do not have basic information about the charges and what the police say the examinee did, you will not be able to interview the examinee to determine appreciation of the charges and a grasp of what the police claim the examinee did. The questions can be asked, of course, but you will not be able to probe the examinee's answer without knowing how far off the examinee's answer might be.

Legal History

The examiner should try to obtain some information about the examinee's past contacts with the legal system. This may be helpful in understanding the examinee's later concerns about the future legal process or making judgments about malingering (e.g., when examinees' experience suggests that they should have much better understanding of the process than they claim to have). Prosecuting and defense attorneys sometimes can be helpful in obtaining legal history information.

Clinical History

Records of past psychiatric inpatient admissions and other mental health services should be obtained whenever possible. Their absence will almost always create difficulties in interviewing and in formulating the case. Diagnostic issues often become clearer when one knows the person's history of need for mental health services, as well as the observations of the examinee by other mental health professionals in other circumstances.

Collateral Information from Outside Parties

Most competence evaluations are enhanced by some contact—often by telephone—with various individuals who have first-hand acquaintance with the examinee. Speaking with the examinee's attorney can clarify problem behaviors that the attorney has observed in interviews with his or her client. But often it is helpful to contact parties outside the legal process as well. For example, family members, treating clinicians, and teachers may offer important observations about the examinee's behavior in everyday life that corroborates or contradicts impressions obtained in examinee interviews and records.

SCOPE AND SETTING OF EVALUATIONS

A number of factors influence where and when examiners perform their competence evaluations. Hospitalization during the competence evaluation is required in some jurisdictions. During the 1980s and 1990s, however, the majority of jurisdictions moved toward arrangements that avoid the added time and expense of inpatient evaluations whenever possible (discussed further in Chapter 7). Screening evaluations, and full competence evaluations of examinees who are not hospitalized, typically are performed in jails, outpatient forensic centers, or private practitioners' offices.

You may sometimes encounter problems in the physical arrangements for your interview or testing of examinees. Jails and detention centers are not clinics and often do not have offices that were designed for the types of evaluations that you do. One accommodates to these conditions within reason. But sometimes the conditions are so cramped, hot, or open to visual/auditory distractions that the results of the evaluation are likely to be unreliable. In such situations, you should make it known to those in control that doing your evaluation in this setting will risk acquiring poor information for the judge who has asked for your evaluation and opinion.

Many jurisdictions have established (by statute or court policy) that the report must be submitted to the court within a certain period of time. Often this is 30 or 60 days, but some jurisdictions have shorter time periods. Most jurisdictions also have a rule that allows for the time to be extended (e.g., for another 30 days) in very difficult cases or when certain records that are crucial to the case cannot be obtained within the allowable time. You should begin seeking the records and background information for the evaluation as soon after you receive the referral as possible. Set a reasonable date for the interview with the examinee that will allow you to review these records before that time.

ACCOUNTABILITY

Standards of accountability for forensic evaluations are high. Documentation of every step in the evaluation is important and generally should be done with greater care than in routine clinical practice.

PRODUCING A RECORD

The data you collect are legal evidence. Later you might have to account for every contact, verify every fact, and demonstrate how each test score was calculated. Therefore, it is helpful to maintain a detailed written record of every step in the procedure. The record should include dates and contents of every contact with attorneys and the examinee. It should include phone numbers and start-end times for every telephone conversation with other parties throughout the evaluation process. It may include dates of entry and exit for jail visits, as well as the length of time for each interview. It should reflect each method used, the raw data for examinees' verbal responses to interview and test items, and the time and sequence of the various methods. Test scores should be recorded clearly on standard test forms and double-checked for clerical or judgment errors. Records should reflect the dates and destinations of all reports or other communications made regarding the results.

ATTORNEY NOTIFICATION AND PRESENCE TO MONITOR THE EVALUATION

Another type of accountability arises when the examinee's attorney is present at the evaluation interview. Some jurisdictions provide the right for an examinee's attorney to be present during the examinee's session with the examiner. In other jurisdictions it is a matter of court or examiner discretion. The *Specialty Guidelines for Forensic Psychology* (American Psychology-Law Society and American Academy of Forensic Psychology, 2011) urges that examiners should notify the examinee's attorney that the evaluation is taking place before contact with the examinee occurs. This provides the attorney an opportunity to raise objections to the evaluation or simply to know the evaluation has begun. Notifying by telephone is typical. If the attorney is not in the office, leave a voice message. Unless local rules say otherwise, you can proceed to do a court-ordered evaluation for competence to stand trial without the attorney's approval as long as you have given the attorney notification.

Attorneys occasionally say that they want to be present at the interview. They may have various intentions or motives (e.g., to learn more about their client, to protect the client from saying things that might jeopardize the client's interests, or to document the questions asked so that the attorney can better use or challenge the content of the interviews).

Whether or not the state provides this right, typically you should simply make the necessary arrangements with the attorney. Many examiners are concerned that the presence of the attorney may influence the examinee's behavior in ways that will reduce the quality of the data obtained. It is perfectly acceptable for the examiner to negotiate this with the attorney (e.g., "This will be fine, as long as you sit in the back of the room behind your client and do not speak. Just raise your hand if you are concerned about something your client is going to say."). You can adjust the agreement if necessary. For example, you can ask the attorney to leave the room during certain tests if you believe that the attorney's presence violates standardization and therefore would render the test results invalid. If the attorney becomes intrusive and is difficult to manage, you can simply discontinue the interview. Politely indicate that you will be telling the court that you could not complete the competence interview and that you will be explaining why.

AUDIOTAPING THE EVALUATION

You may wish to consider audiotaping your evaluation sessions with examinees, and some authorities have even urged consideration of videotaping. Recording data electronically sometimes can be helpful in clarifying specific details of the procedure raised at the competence hearing. In addition, audiotape recording relieves the examiner from detailed note-taking during the examination, and it provides a convenient record for the examiner's review during subsequent scoring and interpretation.

There are other matters to consider, however. Few courts require this level of documentation, and in very few cases would the tape be used as evidence. Moreover, many jails and other settings in which evaluations will be performed have rules against bringing any electronic equipment into the facility. Finally, audiotaping sometimes might have a negative effect on the data one obtains; it can be inhibiting for some examinees, and not much is known about its influence on the results of standardized testing.

DEFENDANT PREPARATION

Ethical obligations (and laws in many states) require that the examinee must be informed of the nature of the competence evaluation before the examinee is interviewed. This obligation is meant to ensure that the examinee knows that the evaluation has legal purposes, not traditional clinical objectives, and that there are limits to confidentiality and privilege in the relationship.

In most states, proceeding to engage in a competence to stand trial evaluation requires only that the examinee be informed, not that the examinee provide informed consent. "Informed consent" requires competence to make the consent decision. To require it would create the odd situation of never being able to evaluate examinees' competence to stand trial unless they were competent (which would require an evaluation of their competence to decide on their participation).

One could argue that this leaves examinees open to potential jeopardy, given that they might not have the capacity to understand the implications of their participation. If they do not comprehend the purposes of the evaluation (e.g., that it is not a confidential conversation with an ordinary doctor), they might say something about the alleged offense that would be against their interest when a court considers evidence for their crime. Shouldn't the evaluation require a competent waiver of the right to silence?

This is not necessary in most states, because their statutes (or case law) provide legal protection that limits how the competence evaluation results may be used. Information obtained in competence to stand trial evaluations typically cannot be entered into evidence in any other hearing in the adjudicative process on any matters other than competence. In addition, in many jurisdictions, examiners are instructed not to include in their competence report or testimony any information that the examinee provided that might be self-incriminating. As long as one or both of these protections applies in your jurisdiction, proceeding without "informed" consent (competent consent) is allowed and ethical.

What information should the examinee be provided? The following are the most important points to convey in preparing an examinee for a court-ordered competence evaluation, and they should be offered in language that the examinee is most likely to understand:

- **Purpose:** That the purpose is to determine what the examinee understands about trials and whether the examinee is prepared to work with his or her attorney
- **Court-ordered:** That you are doing the evaluation at the request of the court (judge)
- **Who you are:** That you are a psychologist or psychiatrist, but that you are not like psychologists and psychiatrists in hospitals or clinics because you are not the examinee's doctor
- **Limits of confidentiality:** That you will be reporting your results to the court (judge), and therefore the interview and its results are not confidential. However, you will be reporting your results *only* to the judge or to others the judge indicates, not to other people outside the court, and in this sense you will respect the examinee's privacy.
- **Choice:** That the examinee can choose whether to participate in the interview, but that you will be doing an evaluation and reporting your results to the court, with or without the examinee's participation

Private competence evaluations requested by the defense ordinarily will be protected by privilege within the attorney-client relationship. The prosecution is likely to see the results only if the defense decides to enter the evaluation as evidence in the competence hearing. But there are some exceptions to this. For example, if the defense seeks competence evaluations from more than one examiner and decides to introduce only one of them into evidence, the others might well be open to subpoena.

All of the above advice requires adjustment, however, if you are asked to perform the competence evaluation in the context of a broader evaluation that addresses other forensic questions as well. In some courts, it is rather common to get requests to perform "dual purpose evaluations" involving assessment of competence to stand trial and criminal responsibility evaluation at the same time. This changes the requirements for preparing the examinee. In a *court-ordered* evaluation that also includes criminal responsibility, the purpose must be extended ("... and your mental state at the time of the alleged offense"). The limits of confidentiality might be stated differently ("Concerning your mental state at the time of the alleged offense, that information will only be heard by the court if your lawyer decides to use it"). And greater emphasis should be placed on the examinee's right to decide not to report anything surrounding the time of the offense.

CONDUCTING THE EVALUATION WITH THE DEFENDANT

There is no established sequence for collecting data in competence evaluations. This is a matter of examiner discretion and is likely to vary with the methods that have been selected. A typical approach is represented in the following discussion. It does not follow the same sequence as the five objectives outlined earlier.

INQUIRY ABOUT BACKGROUND AND HISTORY

Begin with a brief inquiry into the examinee's background and social history, as well as his or her present status and living conditions (e.g., length of time in confinement, current living arrangements). Most examiners then obtain a brief life history. This typically includes very basic information about the examinee's family (during the examinee's childhood), extent of education and any educational problems, military service, marriages, occupational history, health problems and head injuries, and psychiatric hospitalizations.

Included in this brief review is whatever the examinee wishes to provide about past contacts with the legal system. The objective here is not to review each arrest and offense, but rather to learn the degree to which the examinee has some experience with legal proceedings and their purpose (which may be relevant later when assessing the examinee's competence abilities). Ask especially about the examinee's contacts with attorneys in past cases. Remember that the examinee's experience with attorneys cannot be determined on the basis of the number of arrests. Many arrests do not lead to appointment of an attorney.

CLINICAL INQUIRY

Many examiners then proceed to whatever methods they plan to use to assess evidence for psychopathology, developmental disability, or other characteristics that may be relevant for managing the Causal objective of the evaluation. This is when the examiner would potentially use any of the methods described under the Causal objective in Chapter 3: a formal mental status exam, a structured diagnostic interview, and/or psychological testing. Included here are the potential use of tests of malingering of mental or intellectual disability, especially if the information obtained by this point—from interview or collateral records—begins to raise suspicions.

INQUIRY ABOUT CURRENT ALLEGED OFFENSE

Inquiry then can proceed to the examinee's report of current legal circumstances (e.g., what the police say that the examinee did and the examinee's brief description of events before, during, and after the alleged offense). The purpose of this is not to get details or to challenge the examinee. What the examinee did or did not do is not particularly relevant for the competence question. The purpose is simply to learn whether the examinee can provide this type of information in a manner that the examiner can understand. Recall that part of the purpose is to determine the examinee's "ability to communicate with counsel." Being able to give a coherent description of the event is part of that ability.

Some attorneys might object to the examiner asking the examinee to recount events during the alleged offense. The attorney might be concerned about the examinee making self-incriminating statements, despite the fact that in most states the examinee's statements about the alleged offense cannot be admitted as evidence in hearings other than the competence hearing. If the attorney strongly objects to the examinee offering a description of the events during the alleged offense, you can go forward without such observations by changing your strategy. The examinee's ability to communicate things often can be judged on the basis of the examinee's discussion of other matters during the interview. For example, some examiners ask the examinee to begin describing what happened a couple of days ago, beginning when the examinee got out of bed. What time was it? What is the first thing the examinee did? What was for breakfast? And what was the examinee thinking or talking about during breakfast? And so on. This can provide evidence of potential problems in sequencing of information, confused recall of events, and verbal communication skills, which is a large part of what you hoped to learn by asking the examinee to describe the events surrounding the alleged offense.

ASSESSING COMPETENCE ABILITIES

Inquiry then turns to a "competence abilities interview" designed to assess directly the functional abilities associated with the standard for competence to stand trial. The previous discussion of events around the time of the alleged offense usually flows easily into the abilities interview, because typically it begins with, "Let's talk about your present situation. What are your charges? What do they call the thing they say you did?"

As described in Chapter 3, there are a number of standardized tools that can be used to assess abilities relevant for competence to stand trial. Some examiners do not use tools, preferring to engage in their own semi-structured, nonstandardized interview. Many examiners fashion their questions around the items in the *Competency Assessment Instrument* described in Chapter 3, or they develop their own questions based on lists of items such as those in Appendix C. With juveniles, examiners sometimes employ the structured interview by Grisso (2005) called the JACI (see Chapter 3).

When you use standardized competence tools, you should always supplement them with a more focused exploratory interview regarding the examinee's understanding or belief about specific trial-related matters. The reasons for this were discussed in Chapter 3. None of the tools cover all of the specific abilities that one wants to examine. And the nomothetic tools often do not get at the more individualized ways in which examinees' deficits are manifested.

Inquiry About Understanding

The interview typically begins with questions to explore the examinee's factual Understanding of the charges, pleas, how a plea agreement works, possible penalties, participants in the process, and other matters pertaining to the trial process. This is a good place to start, because the remaining abilities that are assessed often rely on basic understanding of these matters. A review of some of the Understanding items in standardized tools will help you see the range of items that should be asked in the Understanding inquiry. (See Appendix C for examples in the CAI.)

During questions about factual Understanding, some examinees may perform inadequately not because of a present *inability* to understand trial matters, but merely because they do not possess necessary information: they have not been exposed to it or, if they were, did not learn it. In cases in which this is suspected, some examiners employ a "teach and retest" strategy during or immediately after the Understanding items. (Note also that competence ability instruments described in Chapter 3 sometimes have these procedures as part of their standardized design.)

A "teach and retest" procedure involves instructing an examinee in some of the basic matters that were misunderstood or seemed to be understood only vaguely. Then the examiner asks questions to determine whether the examinee can recall the information accurately. For example, "So that's what lawyers do. Now, tell me in your own words... what's the purpose of lawyers in a trial? How would you describe that to someone?" Some examiners do the "retest" immediately after teaching the examinee the relevant information. Yet many examinees (especially juveniles) might be able to respond adequately on short-term recall yet have little capacity to retain the information for use later in the trial process. Therefore, it is important to do another "retest" later, either at the end of the evaluation session or at a second session a few days later.

Inquiry About Appreciation

Sufficient questions should be asked to explore how examinees apply what they know to their own situation, or whether they can use what they know when presented with examples. Ways to do this can be found in most of the standardized tools. Sometimes examiners ask these questions in conjunction with Understanding items. For example, "What is the role of the judge?" (Examinee: "He runs the trial. He's supposed to make sure everything is fair.") "Okay, let's imagine you are in your trial for these charges—would you expect the judge to be fair?" (Yes or no.) "What makes you think that?" Similarly, after inquiry about the role of a defendant's lawyer: "How about your lawyer? What do you expect your lawyer to do when you talk together and when she represents you in court?" Other examiners reserve this type of questioning until all the Understanding inquiry has been completed. Note that the focus changes from "what is supposed to happen" to "what do you believe will happen in your case?"

Standardized tools offer examples of other ways to do this, especially by providing brief hypothetical questions that ask examinees to use what they know in some context. For example, "Let's imagine that your lawyer asks you to tell her exactly what happened that night. Why would she want to know that?" Notice that this type of question provides opportunities for an examinee's distorted or faulty beliefs to influence the answer. For example, "So that the lawyer will know whether to defend me or not—they only defend you if you are innocent." Or, "She's just trying to nail me—she's acting like she wants to help, but she can't fool me—I know that she's really got something going with the prosecutor."

Inquiry About Reasoning

The point of this inquiry is to assess examinees' abilities to process information about a decision. One of the most common decisions that examinees have to make is a pleading decision. Sometimes pleading decisions are made in the context of a plea agreement—an offer by the prosecutor to the defense attorney that the prosecutor will ask the court for a lesser penalty if the examinee pleads guilty. A hypothetical vignette about a plea agreement, therefore, is the most common method for assessing the defendant's ability to process information to make a trial-relevant decision.

Such vignettes typically describe a defendant charged with a particular offense, then describe the conditions of a plea agreement in which some lesser penalty is offered for a guilty plea. It also describes the greater possible penalty if one pleads not guilty but is found guilty. The examinee is asked about the pros and cons of pleading guilty, and the pros and cons of pleading not guilty. The examiner at some point asks, "How would you make this decision?" or "Which do you think you might decide to do?" and "What makes that seem best?" Note that the examinee's actual choice is not what is being assessed, because examinees are free to choose whatever they want, no matter how odd the choice might seem to others. The examiner is observing whether the examinee's reasoning about the decision becomes confused, whether the examinee can manage the process of balancing pros and cons, and whether the choice makes sense given the examinee's own logic. The examiner is observing this with a clinical eye as well, considering whether the types of confusion the examinee manifests might be related to various cognitive disabilities (e.g., memory, deficits in abstract thinking, intellectual deficits, and sometimes delusional ideas).

Inquiry About Communication and Trial Participation

In one sense, the examiner is observing the examinee's capacities for communication with legal counsel throughout the interview. This involves using the examinee's responses to any of the examiner's questions to judge their clarity, the examinee's ability to say on task, and the relevance or irrelevance of the examinee's responses in light of the content of the examiner's questions. Direct questions about the examinee's experience in talking to his or her own lawyer (if the examinee and lawyer have met) are often helpful as well.

The examinee's participation in a court hearing, if it occurs, is also of concern in competence evaluations. Can the examinee attend well enough to grasp what is being said during a trial? Would the examinee be able to testify if that were necessary? Can the examinee manage his or her behavior during the court hearing so that proceedings can be maintained in a manner that is fair to the examinee?

Examinees' abilities in this area often are less a matter of what they know or believe and more related to their degree of emotional control. Most examiners do ask examinees whether they know how one is supposed to comport themselves in trials, and what they should do if they hear something that they think isn't true ("Don't yell out—quietly tell your lawyer"). But interpretations of these data also are based on the examiner's broader clinical observations about the examinee's degree of impulse control, degree of fear and anxiety in the face of stress, and other clinical and emotional features of the examinee.

SPECIAL CONSIDERATIONS IN COMPETENCE EVALUATIONS OF JUVENILES

The general process described in this chapter applies as well to competence evaluations of juveniles as to adults. Juveniles' evaluations, however, require some modifications or additions to the process.

PARENT INTERVIEWS

Many evaluations of adult examinees involve interviews only with the defendant. In contrast, most clinicians who perform juvenile competence evaluations interview parents or other caregivers as well. There are two reasons. Parents often can provide information about health, educational, and behavioral problems that young people are less likely to want to or be able to provide. The other reason is that parents usually are directly involved in their children's decisions about pleas, plea agreements, and other choices that defendants must make. Sometimes that involvement can be helpful, but often children's and adolescents' already-questionable capacities are undermined by parents' intrusiveness or their own failures to understand the legal process. This sometimes provides important information about the context in which the youth must function (the Interactive objective in Chapter 2). Typically the examiner interviews the young person and parent together for a brief time, then the parent alone, then the young person alone for the offense, clinical and functional abilities inquiries.

Be aware that parents cannot make decisions for their children in delinquency or criminal cases, and they cannot overrule their children's decisions as defendants. Whatever their age, defendants must make their choices independently, because legal doctrine holds that no one but the defendant can waive important constitutional rights. This is a legal requirement that at first may seem contrary to the notion that adolescents are not fully mature and are still appropriately under the guardianship of their parents. Yet there are often cases in which a parent's decision or advice might be based on a conflict of interest that creates an injustice (e.g., when a parent advises or tells a youth to confess and plead guilty, largely because the alternative suspect in the alleged incidence is likely to be the father, whose incarceration would endanger the future of the whole family).

MULTIPLE SESSIONS

Many adult competence evaluations involve only one lengthy session with the examinee or an interview session and a testing session. Most forensic examiners skilled in juvenile competence evaluations attempt to see their examinees for multiple interviews, typically two. There are many reasons for this. Adolescents' moods are often labile, changing considerably even in a few days. They are also more reactive to new situations, often being quieter or more oppositional in initial meetings and (if not threatened in that initial contact) somewhat more open in a second meeting. Thus, a second session often reveals something more or different about a young person than the first session would have suggested. In addition, young people's diagnostic conditions often are more challenging because, in general, adolescents' disorders are less differentiated than those of adults. For example, symptoms typically associated with mood disorders and anxiety disorders tend to coexist in adolescence, making differential diagnosis more difficult. Multiple sessions are often needed to gather the necessary clinical information to narrow the diagnostic options.

DATA COLLECTION METHODS

Competence evaluations with young people will, of course, require the use of different measures of psychopathology, personality, and intelligence or achievement than would be used in adult cases. In addition, examiners using structured competence ability tools described in Chapter 3 must recognize that currently there are no adolescent norms for these tools. They can still be used but with certain cautions. Adolescents' performance on them can be compared to that of adult norms. But some courts employ an "age-peer" approach to determining whether a young person's abilities are sufficient for juvenile court proceedings. The absence of juvenile norms on these tools decreases their value in those circumstances.

DEVELOPMENTAL HISTORY

The "Background and History" inquiry described earlier typically requires more detailed information about early development than would be acquired for adult cases. This is because adolescents' deficits often are related to their less-mature cognitive development. Thus the evaluation with young people often involves inquiry into early developmental milestones, illnesses, head injuries, and details of educational progress and Individual Educational Plans (required by schools when young people have been identified as having intellectual, learning, or behavioral disabilities). All of these may be of importance when interpreting their deficits in competence abilities to meet the Causal objective of competence evaluations.

AFTER THE EVALUATION SESSION

The data obtained in contact with the examinee may create new questions for which more information is needed. For example, the examinee's apparent psychopathology may raise the need to obtain past mental health records that the examiner learned about from the examinee. Clinical hypotheses might have been developed that require psychological or neuropsychological testing of greater length than can be accomplished in this first evaluation session, so that one or more additional evaluation sessions might need to be scheduled. Examinees sometimes describe events—such as their experiences with their attorney—that can be checked for their accuracy by contacting others who may be aware of those events.

Examinees' evaluations sometimes raise serious questions about their mental status or future behavior quite apart from the issue of their competence to stand trial. For example, they may be in need of immediate hospitalization for their own protection. Sometimes examinees inform examiners of their plans to harm someone, raising questions of danger to third parties in the immediate future. How should the examiner respond to these questions that were not the focus of the referral?

When the competence evaluation is performed privately (at the request of defense counsel), the proper response is to report them to the examinee's attorney without delay (that is, without waiting to complete one's evaluation report). When the evaluation is court-ordered, the examiner usually should report the matter to the examinee's attorney and to the court. To do so does not violate confidentiality or privilege, because efforts were made by the examiner to inform the examinee that what was learned in the evaluation would be shared with the court. Risk of harm to others should be reported only if the danger is imminent and focused (e.g., the examinee who describes a crime that he or she plans to execute in coming days or weeks that is likely to harm a specific person).

Having collected the data, we now proceed to their interpretation to address the referral question. This is discussed in Chapter 5. Of course, the process of data collection and interpretation are not quite that distinct in actual practice. Most examiners are beginning to form their potential interpretations while data are being collected. Indeed, this often stimulates them to seek additional data to confirm and disconfirm competing interpretations.

Chapter 5

INTERPRETING THE DATA

This chapter provides suggestions and guidelines for interpreting your data in ways that are relevant to assist the court in addressing competence to stand trial. The complexity of the interpretive process does not lend itself to description by any fixed set of rules. No particular fact or observation ever leads invariably to any single interpretation by itself. The clinician considers the data set as a whole, so that any score or other observation may have somewhat different significance depending on the presence or absence of other factors.

The following sections describe common problems encountered in the process, tips for improving inferences and avoiding misinterpretations, and brief case examples of interpretations in competence evaluations. Once again, we will use the five objectives of competence evaluations as our outline.

FUNCTIONAL OBJECTIVE: INFERENCES ABOUT TYPE AND DEGREE OF DEFICITS IN COMPETENCE ABILITIES

When all data have been collected, a logical place for the examiner to begin the review of the data is with the question, "What are the types and degrees of functional deficits in the defendant's competence abilities?" Some examples of this process will be provided in this section. Let's begin with a reminder of the basic concepts first described in Chapters 1 and 2 that can structure the examiner's inquiry into deficits in the defendant's functional abilities.

Chapter 1 provided a legal basis for defining the types of abilities that are relevant for competence to stand trial. It pointed out that the *Dusky* standard for competence to stand trial specifically refers to two types of understanding: factual understanding and rational understanding. The standard also refers to the ability to assist counsel, which has been interpreted to include a variety of functions associated psychologically with communication and reasoning. Finally, other legal authority (e.g., the U.S. Supreme Court in *Godinez v. Moran*) asserts that defendants must be able to make various decisions that might arise in the adjudicative process (e.g., deciding how to plead, and how to respond to potential plea agreements).

Chapter 2 described two ways to classify problems in competence abilities. One is to use the *Dusky* standard's "factual understanding"—knowing the important things about charges, participant roles, and trial processes—and "rational understanding," which would include the other two types of deficits in the above paragraph.

The other way, which we will use in this chapter, is to employ the "UARC" concepts. This conceptual framework sorts deficits into *Understanding* ("factual understanding") and two types of "rational understanding:" Appreciation and Reasoning. *Appreciation* is used to classify deficits involving the interference of faulty beliefs with the application of what one understands (often due to delusions, rigid psychological defenses, or developmental immaturity). *Reasoning* refers to deficits involved in the processing of information when making decisions (e.g., an apparent cognitive inability to manage the complexity of a plea agreement). *Communication* deficits focus on receiving and conveying information in the defendant's interaction with legal counsel or with others in the court process.

Let's briefly "rehearse" the distinction between the U, A, and R concepts before we consider the various ways in which they are manifested. Imagine that a defendant seems to know most of what is needed regarding the charges and penalties, is able to identify the basic roles of all of the participants in an adjudicative process, knows what a plea agreement is, and so forth. The defendant may seem to have adequate *Understanding*. Yet this defendant might manifest a deficit in *Appreciation* (e.g., understanding that "A judge is someone who makes fair decisions," yet believing that in his or her own case those facts will not apply because "Judge Smith has been bought by the C.I.A."). Or in another case, the defendant may understand most of the important elements of trials, yet manifest serious deficits in *Reasoning* (e.g., becoming extremely confused when trying to process the advantages and disadvantages of a plea agreement in her own case).

One of the most fundamental errors that some examiners make in competence to stand trial cases is to focus on Understanding while missing or neglecting possible deficits of the Appreciation or Reasoning type. Understanding is indeed basic. If it is seriously impaired, then by itself it will decrease the likelihood that the defendant can engage in decision making and other important roles as a defendant in a trial process. *Yet factual Understanding is best seen as a "threshold question."* If a defendant manifests serious deficits in Understanding, that in itself is sometimes enough to tip the balance toward a finding of incompetence. But if the defendant "passes" the Understanding threshold, there is still much more to consider. Do not make the mistake of concluding that defendants are "competent" merely because they can accurately describe to you most of what defendants are supposed to "know" about charges, penalties, pleas, roles of participants, and the trial process.

The following subsections provide some examples of issues that arise at this descriptive level of the competence analysis. In the following discussion, we will capitalize the terms Understanding, Appreciation, and Reasoning when we use them as classes of competence abilities.

DEFICITS IN UNDERSTANDING

Some of the standardized, normed instruments for assessing competence abilities provide examiners with scoring criteria that define whether a defendant's Understanding is "deficient" or "adequate." Some also provide norms that suggest whether a defendant's score on a factual understanding scale is significantly different in relation to past research samples of competent and incompetent defendants. Examiners who employ nonstandardized competence ability interviews, however, will sometimes have difficulty deciding whether or not a defendant's response to some questions about trials does or does not represent a "deficit." This difficulty takes several forms.

Some defendants may give vague but not incorrect responses to basic questions in a competence interview. For example:

> *Defendant Adam* said that the job of his attorney was "to help me." But he could not elaborate further on the attorney's role or function in the trial process.

Adam has the very simplest level of understanding, but his answer provides no indication of the kind of "help" offered in the client-attorney relation. We would have been more confident if Adam had responded to the examiner's additional inquiry: "He's supposed to help get me off" or "He's on my side in the trial" or even "He'll explain things to me." "Help me" does not distinguish the attorney from many other people, including probation officers, judges in some courts, and even police officers. Later in the pretrial process, what if Adam would announce that he didn't like his lawyer and wanted to proceed without one? We could surely question whether he is adequately prepared to make this decision based on his "help me" response to the examiner's question about "the job of the attorney."

Here is another example of a defendant's vague response, partly because of the examiner's way of asking the question:

> *Defendant Benny* was asked, "When a person pleads to a charge of having done something, what are the pleas the person can make?" Benny said, "Guilty or not guilty." When the clinician asked, "What does it mean when you make those pleas?" Benny said, "Guilty means you did it and not guilty means you didn't." The examiner asked also about a plea of "not guilty by reason of insanity." Benny said that meant, "You did it but you were crazy when you did it." The examiner concluded that Benny had a basic understanding of the potential pleas he could decide to offer in response to the allegations.

Did he? His answers do not suggest that he understands that he can decide which way to plead. His answers would have been perfect if the question had been, "What are the possible *verdicts*?" But nothing in his answers indicates that Benny knows that in "making a plea" the defendant decides whether or not to offer the court an admission of guilt. A plea of not guilty does not mean what Benny said: that is, that you didn't do it. Pleading not guilty means that you *say* you didn't do it. We would have been more confident if he had said, "A plea of not guilty means you deny the charges and they have to prove it if they are going to find you guilty." Without something more than Benny provided, we cannot conclude that he understood that a plea is a decision about what to tell the court when you are accused. The examiner probably would have obtained the relevant additional data if he had first asked, "What do we mean by a plea?" and later, "What *happens* when you plead guilty? And when you plead not guilty?"

Some cases raise the question of "how much" a defendant needs to know so that Understanding is considered adequate.

> *Defendant Carla* described a jury as "the people who listen to all the stuff in court and then they go and decide whether or not you committed the crime. They go in with an open mind, and they decide and come out and tell the judge." But when the examiner asked her how juries do that, she said, "I don't really know. It must be hard. They'd have to remember everything and talk a lot about it. I suppose they'd have to pray about it a lot...try to get the Lord to help them decide what's right. God is the only one who really knows the truth, and God is just. He wouldn't let a guilty person go free."

As long as Carla understands basically what the jury does, is this last bit of information important in deciding whether her Understanding is adequate? Does she have to understand *how* juries make decisions, and does her embellishment about a jury's prayerful process of deliberation make a difference?

She says they must "remember everything," which implies that they listen to the evidence. Perhaps that is enough. Typically courts do not require a particularly sophisticated or technical level of Understanding of the adjudicative process and rules of law. For example, defendants need not be able to anticipate all possible strategies that might be available to argue against the charges. It is presumed that defendants will be instructed by their lawyers when necessary regarding more detailed aspects of the law, especially in matters of defense strategy. If Carla had been asked what it meant to "appeal" a case and appeared not to understand it, a court probably would not have considered this a meaningful deficit weighing against competence.

Yet we would have reason to be uncertain in Carla's instance. For example, is it possible that her notion about a prayerful jury in touch with God, together with her own feelings of guilt, could play a significant role in her pleading decision one way or the other? We need to know more. Perhaps this belief that juries ask for God's help is a vague idea that could be corrected by informing her that this is not how juries make decisions. If so, we could consider it less important for purposes of conclusions about her adequate Understanding. It is easily remedied. But what if this is the first sign of an underlying set of more enduring beliefs about God's hand in the trial process? Imagine that Carla also has a history of clinical depressions during which she sees herself as sinful and undeserving. Imagine that as the interview proceeded, her references to God's justice appeared repeatedly and began to look like a fixed delusional idea far exceeding the ordinarily religious person's idea about the role of God in the legal process. What may have seemed a relatively insignificant deficit in Understanding might become a significant problem in Appreciation.

DEFICITS IN APPRECIATION

As noted earlier, Understanding is a threshold issue; if it is not adequate, it may be a sufficient basis for a finding of incompetence. But if it is adequate, there are further things to consider that may yet suggest deficits that could result in a finding of incompetence. One of these is failures in Appreciation. Most failures in Appreciation consist of false, fixed beliefs (sometimes delusional) or rigidly held presumptions that are not easily changed by efforts to challenge them. They impair the rational use of what the defendant understands in the process of working with counsel or making decisions:

> *Defendant Danny,* his attorney reported, "is impossible to work with . . . he just stares at me, makes strange faces, and won't talk." The examiner noted that Danny did stare at him strangely a few times early in the evaluation. Yet he answered questions and demonstrated very few deficits in his comprehension of the nature of the trial, the charges, the possible outcomes, and roles of the participants. When the examiner asked Danny what he thought about *his* lawyer, Danny explained that "I looked in her soul and I saw the serpent." Danny firmly believed that exactly one-half of the people in the world worked "the devil's influence," and that he had the power to identify them by looking deep into their eyes "to their soul-center." References to this delusional belief also were found in clinical notes of his hospitalization several months prior to his arrest on the present offense.

Other failures in Appreciation, however, are misinterpretations that may or may not be delusional, but represent a fixed belief or attitude that could have serious impact on defendants' abilities to use factual Understanding when applied to their situation:

> *Defendant Elaine* seemed to understand the basic functions of judges when she described them as "making sure everything in court is done

> the way it's supposed to be done... he stops and starts everything... if you're guilty, he decides how much time you have to do." Later in the interview, however, Elaine mentioned that she wished she could have hired a private lawyer instead of relying on a public defender. When asked why, she observed (correctly) that this meant that everyone (the defense attorney, prosecutor, and judge) was paid by the "government." When questioned about the significance of this, Elaine launched into a well-articulated lecture on the government's intrusion into people's everyday lives, emphasizing that the government was not "of, by, or for the people," and that the country had completely abandoned the form of democracy that the founders intended. Courts were part of government, thus courts were sometimes corrupt and fairness uncertain. Elaine had no history of mental disorder, but she was known to be an active, vocal and long-term member of a libertarian organization.

Does this "count" when making interpretations about Elaine's competence or incompetence to stand trial? Most states' laws identify mental disorder, developmental disability, or developmental immaturity as the necessary causes for incompetence, and Elaine meets none of those criteria. But we are not at that step in our interpretations. The sole purpose at the moment (the Functional objective) is to identify deficits that might work to her disadvantage when making decisions in the trial process. Our data indicate that she has a rigid belief that may have that effect. For now, we simply classify it as a problem in Appreciation, and later we will deal with its implications for meeting legal criteria for competence.

> *Defendant Falaya,* a 14-year-old, said her lawyer was "a person to help you... tries to prove you're innocent... tells your story in court ... makes sure you don't get screwed." Falaya said she could trust her lawyer, and when asked what she could do to help the lawyer in her case, she said it was important to tell the truth, "because if you don't she don't know how to deal with things." The examiner almost proceeded to other matters, because these answers clearly were enough to signify substantial Understanding of an attorney's role. But she decided to check on the meaning of Falaya's last comment. Falaya's reply: "If you didn't do it, she needs to know where you were instead and like that. If you did do it, she needs to know that, too, so she can decide whether to be on your side." The examiner discovered that Felaya had a faulty belief about counsel that rendered her adequate Understanding moot: "Lawyers help kids if they're innocent, right? I mean, if your lawyer thought you did it, she'd have to tell the judge.

> She couldn't stand there and lie about it to the judge." Further inquiry indicated that Falaya could not imagine it any other way. "How could adults lie to adults? Aren't they all supposed to be helping kids?"

Perhaps Falaya's belief can be modified fairly easily so that this Appreciation question turns out to be a problem of Understanding. But what if we find that in many areas of her life, Falaya's development is somewhat delayed for a 14-year-old, so that she often demonstrates thinking that is more typical of preadolescent "concrete operations" than "formal operations?" Her everyday world has taught her that her life as a child is controlled by adults, that adults represent authority, and that all adults share in that authority. It is a bit beyond her current abilities to form an abstract notion of "justice" apart from authority, so that it is not in her world view to imagine that as a child she can have the aid of an adult to defy authority. This is a problem of Appreciation that interferes with her rational use of what she knows when making decisions about her legal case.

DEFICITS IN REASONING

Recall that Reasoning refers to abilities involved in the processing of information for making a decision. Sometimes this arises because of defendants' memory problems:

> *Defendant Gerard* appeared to have true amnesia for the events surrounding his alleged offense some 8 months earlier. This was the consequence of a serious head injury sustained at the time. Since then he had undergone considerable rehabilitation. He was alert and responsive during the competence abilities interview and he manifested generally adequate Understanding and no apparent problems in Appreciation. In a second session 2 days later, however, the examiner noted that Gerard had significant difficulty recalling the events of their first session. Moreover, during this second session Gerard's performance on the paired associates portion of the Wechsler Memory Scale (and on other short-term recall tests) indicated that his abilities in this area were far below the level expected on the basis of his other cognitive and intellectual abilities. The examiner began to wonder whether Gerard would be able to recall from day to day the conversations he had with his attorney as well as the events of an eventual trial as they would unfold.

Other cases of impaired Reasoning arise because the defendant is limited in ability to engage in a logical process that involves attention to multiple things at once:

> *Defendant Harold* seemed somewhat limited intellectually. But he was able to grasp most of the things needed for adequate Understanding, and he had no particular beliefs that would distort his use of what he understood. It was when the examiner engaged him in discussing a possible plea agreement that the examiner became concerned. The examiner had explained a number of pros and cons about choosing whether to accept or reject a hypothetical plea agreement. But as Harold began to weigh the options, he got confused. He expressed a preference for certain advantages—like getting the trial over with and not taking risks—but ended up saying he would choose to plead not guilty, even though the advantages he'd endorsed would be the natural consequences of pleading guilty.

His choice was not consistent with what he said he most valued, which led to the examiner's conclusion that his reasoning was not logical. But note closely the examiner's reason for this conclusion. The examiner did not consider whether Harold's choice itself was "wise" or "foolish." The examiner considered the choice illogical because it did not follow from Harold's own expressed values—the consequences that Harold himself said that he desired. "Reasoning" is not faulty because an examinee makes a decision that the examiner thinks is unwise. It is faulty because it does not make sense based on the examinee's own processing of the information.

DEFICITS IN COMMUNICATION

Problems in communication can take various forms. Sometimes they are related to poor Understanding or problems in Appreciation that secondarily have an influence on how the defendant approaches counsel. But others involve a more fundamental inability to relate information to defense counsel in a manner that counsel can use as reliable information for a defense:

> *Defendant Ira* was asked to describe the events on the night that he was arrested. At first he did so in one sentence, which focused mostly on what the alley looked like. As the examiner tried to seek elaboration

("What happened earlier in the evening?" "What happened as you entered the alley?" What happened then?"), Harold's explanation was almost unintelligible as a story, because events that clearly happened after the alleged offense—as well as those that happened before—were related in isolated pieces that did not follow a meaningful sequence. The examiner was not looking for an accurate story, of course, but simply one that allowed others to discern *any* coherent story. Listening to Ira's efforts, which were considerable, never offered that possibility.

These problems in self-expression may have many causes. They can be related to developmental disability (mental retardation), brain syndromes, cognitive disorganization associated with a psychotic disorder, a learning disability, or extreme symptoms of anxiety in social situations. As we have seen throughout this "Functional" discussion, using the UARC scheme to classify deficits usually does not isolate causes of the deficits. That is the Causal objective of the interpretive process.

CAUSAL OBJECTIVE: INFERENCES TO EXPLAIN DEFICITS IN COMPETENCE ABILITIES

Chapter 2 explained that some of the major causes of deficits in competence abilities that need to be explored are mental illnesses, developmental disability (mental retardation), developmental immaturity, and a number of other causes that are not recognized as a basis for incompetence (e.g., dissimulation). You must also explain the connection between any of these causes and the deficits in competence abilities that you have observed. This discussion focuses on this Causal objective.

INFERENCES ABOUT DELUSIONAL BELIEFS

Causal explanations for functional deficits require logical inferences about the connections between the defendant's deficiencies in competence abilities and the clinical condition of the defendant. For example, in cases of schizophrenia, sometimes the defendant's delusional system is manifested in his or her beliefs about the trial process:

Defendant Jasper was arrested for assaulting an airline security guard when a ticket clerk refused to issue Jasper a free airline ticket to Panama. During examination, Jasper repeatedly insisted that the judge's job was to find him guilty or to find the airline guilty. He expected the latter result, since he believed that he had "a God-given right" to a free ticket, and he was certain that the judge would force the airline to give him one. His beliefs were consistent with a psychotic delusion that had a 3-year history, as documented in hospital records and the present examiner's evaluation. In the latest version of the delusion, Jasper had to get to Panama, he said, to begin a mission given him by God that eventually would unite the Western hemisphere "at its umbilical" into a single nation at peace. His delusion caused him to see the trial process as a source of potential vindication for his mission. His own testimony would reveal his mission, he said, and the judge's decision would verify to the world the truth of his calling and would clear the way for his success.

Here is the type of causal argument that the examiner will make to establish the connection between Jasper's mental condition and his competence deficits:

- He currently has a mental disorder (schizophrenia, based on a past history and the examiner's own mental status exam and psychological testing)
- He has an odd and idiosyncratic belief about his appointed purpose in life (the content of the belief)
- The fixed belief is a delusion—that is, a consequence of his mental disorder (past history of the belief's consistency, and clinical knowledge of the nature of delusional beliefs in persons with schizophrenia)
- His deficits in Appreciation are consistent with the delusion (e.g., his grandiose certainty that the court would help him carry out his God-given mission)

Why is this chain of logic needed when the defendant's mental illness and the delusion are so evident? Some defendants have serious symptoms of mental disorder, as well as beliefs that may influence their decisions negatively, yet the two are not related:

Defendant Kinley claimed that there was no use trying to decide about pleading. In planning sessions with his attorney, he seemed depressed, said "It's hopeless...plead me guilty," and responded only minimally to his attorney's belief that a reasonable defense was possible. Kinley

> commented that the judge had "already made up his mind." "It's all arranged," he told the examiner, "no matter how hard my attorney works, the judge, Jury and D.A. are all in it together to get someone like me." His history included occasional psychiatric treatment for depression. Psychological testing found a moderate depressive state (enough to diagnosis Dysthymia), with strong features of alienation, as well as "borderline" developmental disability. The examiner also found that Kinley had a longstanding belief that society worked only for those who were in its conventional mainstream. As a black man accused of raping a white woman, Kinley was convinced that judges and jurors would be controlled by their prejudices, not by the case facts.

Kinley did have symptoms of a mental disorder that were consistent with his pessimism. If his guilty plea was related to his belief that "everyone's out to get me because I am destined to pay for all the sins of the world," the relation between his depressed disorder and this potentially delusional belief might have weighed in favor of incompetence. But his recognition of potential racially related prejudice in the trial presents less of an argument for a finding of incompetence, because it does not seem to be related to his disorder.

INFERENCES ABOUT DEVELOPMENTAL IMMATURITY

When young people have faulty beliefs about trial-related matters, sometimes they are simply extensions of their poor factual Understanding. Other times, however, they are logically related to developmental characteristics of adolescents that are not so easily remediated. The earlier example of Falaya offered that potential interpretation. Here is another:

> *Defendant Larry*, a 15-year-old youth with ADHD, knew that he could go to a juvenile secure facility for several months for the offense with which he was charged. To test whether Larry grasped the significance of this, the examiner asked Larry what was the worst punishment his parents had ever given him. "Clean my room," he said, "I hate to clean my room! I've got to do it when I get home this afternoon." Larry became very worked up at this thought of the day ahead of him, and it was difficult to get him to stop talking about it. After Larry had settled down a bit, the examiner asked him: "So which would you rather do, Larry? Clean your room or go to juvenile detention?" "Detention," Larry said earnestly, "I hate cleaning my room!"

The examiner interpreted Larry's choice as a consequence of his immature tendency (verified by many other sources of information) to respond to decisions by impulsively reacting to his present emotions, rather than considering consequences that were more remote in their possibilities even if they were negative. The examiner related this to Larry's age and his ADHD, demonstrated how it explained many other decisions Larry had made in the past, and showed how it was consistent with many of the illogical decisions that Larry had made when considering his options during the competence interview.

Adolescents' tendency to be influenced by peers and to think idealistically is a possible reason for the following circumstance:

> *Defendant Maria*, a 15-year-old, was facing a plea agreement decision related to her presence at a robbery—she waited in the car—committed by her 20-year-old boyfriend who was convicted earlier in criminal court. The examiner posed a hypothetical plea agreement that would result in probation at home for a year or two if she pled guilty, although the offense could result in a year in a juvenile residential facility if she pled not guilty and was found guilty. At first she said she would probably choose to plead guilty, but after thinking a moment, she changed her mind. "Well, I actually wouldn't care if I went to jail . . . I mean, in a way it would be good, because that's more like what happened to John and if that happened to me then he'd know when we got out that I loved him and he'd like me more."

Sometimes immaturity and psychopathology combine to offer explanations for impaired Appreciation of the significance of one's decisions at trial:

> *Defendant Nate,* a 16-year-old, was charged with murder. He had no delinquency record, a decent school performance, and accomplishments in organized sports. He was dating a girl whom (others said) he "put on a pedestal" and "worshipped," even though she repeatedly taunted him with demeaning remarks. On one of these many occasions, he bludgeoned her. His attorney wanted to make a connection between this event and a history of psychological abuse of Nate by his mother. This was verified by Nate's sister, although there were no earlier Social Service records documenting any abuse. Nate refused this defense strategy, saying that his mother was "perfect" and "shouldn't have to be humiliated for what I did."

The idealization of people with whom Nate was intimately connected was a pattern running through his life—a defense against rejection. In addition, it was augmented by the general tendency of adolescents to think in idealistic ways about their relationships with others.

INFERENCES ABOUT FEIGNING AND MALINGERING

Some defendants attempt to fake poor competence abilities (feigning), while others try to fake symptoms of mental illnesses (malingering). Sometimes they do both. Sometimes defendants do have serious mental disorders (are not malingering), but they attempt to perform more poorly on competence ability interviews than they actually could manage. Examiners try to recognize when these are happening. Chapter 3 described several standardized tools for this purpose. These instruments do not claim to "detect" or "verify" malingering or feigning , but they can often provide additional data to support or contradict that interpretation.

There are a number of excellent references to assist examiners in interpreting data regarding malingering of mental illnesses, neurological disorders, and developmental disabilities. One of these is *Clinical Assessment of Malingering and Deception* (Rogers, 2012). Here we discuss feigning of competence to stand trial deficits.

Some defendants will believe that there is a benefit to being found incompetent to stand trial. They imagine that their charges will be dismissed if they can maintain the appearance of incompetence. Other defendants also expect that the appearance of having "crazy ideas" about the trial process might improve their chances for a later insanity plea.

When testing hypotheses about potential feigning of poor competence abilities, the most useful observation is consistencies or inconsistencies in the defendant's behavior. Suspicion is raised, for example, when a defendant's intellectual capacities or cognitive abilities, as measured by psychological tests, suggest a capacity to comprehend matters better than was manifested in the competence abilities interview. Similarly, the examiner might note an inconsistency between a defendant's poor competence interview performance and the fact that the defendant has had much prior experience with police and courts. Yet this cannot be taken as a hard-and-fast rule. Much research has documented that not all adult or juvenile offenders with frequent experience in court have sophisticated (or even average) knowledge of legal matters.

The examiner should be alert to inconsistencies between the defendant's competence interview performance and the defendant's comments in other parts of the examination:

> *Defendant Opel* claimed ignorance of much of the trial process and its participants, reversed the role of the police and the prosecutor, and offered very confused descriptions of trial evidence. An hour later as the examination was drawing to a close, the examiner (who was asked by the defense attorney to perform the evaluation) asked Opel if there was anything she wished for him to convey to her attorney. “”Yeah,” Opel replied, “tell him I wanta know how things are going.” The examiner asked for specifics, to which she replied, “Among other things, I want to know whether he's looked into getting the confession suppressed.”

INTERACTIVE OBJECTIVE: INFERENCES ABOUT THE SIGNIFICANCE OF DEFICITS

Even when Functional deficits are apparent, they do not always have significance for defendants' trial participation. Their significance depends in part on the defendant's own trial circumstances and whether the defendant's deficits might have a significant impact on the fairness of the trial. Recall the explanation for this objective that was offered in Chapter 2. An inability to calculate arithmetic fractions is a deficit for purposes of altering cooking recipes, but not for playing the violin.

How can examiners assist the court in interpreting deficits with this objective in mind? *The key is to offer an interpretation of the conditions in which the defendant's deficits are likely to have a significant impact on the defendant's performance during a trial, and when they are likely to be less important or significant.* Here is an example of this Interactive approach:

> *Defendant Gerard* was described earlier as having short-term memory problems as a consequence of a head injury. He had trouble remembering things from one interview session to another. The examiner anticipated that Gerard could have difficulty relating the testimony of one witness to that of an earlier witness, or in considering the cu-

> mulative effects of trial evidence at later stages of a trial. This might influence his ability to raise questions to his attorney about inconsistencies he might otherwise have noted across witnesses. But would this necessarily be important for Gerard's trial? Given the data on the pattern of Gerard's memory deficit, the examiner told the court that his memory problems probably would not impair his grasp of the trial process if the trial took no longer than a day. Lack of recall might be a problem, however, if the trial extended to another day or more, requiring recall across more than a 24 hour period of time.

Notice that this explanation did three things. First, the examiner avoided the simplistic explanation that Gerard "could not track the events in a trial." That would not have been true; it would have been a gross overstatement, given the available data. There were no data suggesting he could not remember something a few hours later. Second, the examiner did not try to guess how long the trial would take. Typically examiners are out on a limb if they try to do that. Third, the examiner stated the conditions under which the person's deficits would be more or less likely to be important: "If short, then this . . . if long, then that." The examiner framed the importance of the deficit as "conditional" upon the trial's demands.

Examiners must be careful not to assume the trial circumstances of a defendant and not to factor them into a conclusion about the defendant's competence. The proper form is always *conditional*:

> *Defendant Peter* had no remarkable deficits in Understanding, Appreciation, or Reasoning. But psychological test results and some observations buried in past hospital records indicated that Peter's relationship with his mother had been awful and left him with a tendency to react violently when he was directly confronted by women whom he perceived as "pushy." The examiner knew the female prosecutor who was assigned to the case, and he knew that she would come across in exactly that way. Factoring this trial demand into his interpretations, the examiner felt quite certain that Peter would not be able to control himself when he was cross-examined by the prosecutor. So he told the court that Peter would undoubtedly explode during the trial, for which reason he should be considered incompetent. This caused some confusion and lengthened the hearing as the prosecutor on cross-examination asked question after question about the defendant's everyday behavior, which had never shown any sign of hostility.

The problem in this case was that the examiner did not make a conditional explanation of the prediction. The testimony simply said that Peter might explode because he could not control his temper, failing to refer to the condition: testifying in his own trial, and being cross-examined by a woman. Only after the judge stepped in to ask the examiner directly the reason for this prediction did the examiner describe his logic. In a side-bar conversation, the judge asked the defense attorney whether Peter was likely to be a witness in the trial, and the attorney said it was not likely. The examiner was embarrassed, which could have been avoided if the prediction originally had been stated in simple, conditional form: "If he testifies, then this . . . if he does not, then that."

One of the interesting features of an Interactive perspective is that it sometimes offers suggestions about how to proceed when a defendant has serious deficits in competence abilities. If the relevance of deficits depends on an interaction of the defendant's disability and the demands of the trial, this offers two ways that the court might handle the case. One can *alter the defendant's deficit* so that the defendant can tolerate the demand. This would require a finding of incompetence and development of a remediation plan. Alternatively, one can *change the demands of the situation* to compensate for the defendant's deficit:

> *Defendant Quinta,* age 20, was mildly developmentally disabled, had an auditory handicap, and was extremely dependent and frightened. Pretrial hearings had demonstrated that she was reduced to uncontrollable, loud sobbing under even the least stressful courtroom conditions. This was due in part to her extreme feelings of shame and embarrassment regarding the charges against her, which allegedly involved inappropriate sexual behavior with children whom her neighbors allowed her to babysit. Based on his evaluation, the examiner thought that it was conceivable that Quinta could gain better control of her behavior if given supportive psychotherapy and cognitive behavioral training. He speculated, however that she might gain better control without this treatment if the counselor at her residential school—someone whom Quinta deeply loved and trusted—could sit with her at counsel table. With judicial approval, the hypothesis was tested at the competence hearing. The results were favorable, and the judge did not have to find Quinta incompetent.

CONCLUSORY OBJECTIVE: REACHING A CONCLUSION ABOUT COMPETENCE OR INCOMPETENCE

Chapter 2 indicated that most examiners interpret their findings, then arrive at an opinion that the defendant is competent or incompetent to stand trial. To describe this interpretive process, it is helpful to consider three kinds of cases.

The first includes cases in which the examiner has interpreted the defendant's deficits as likely to be *related to dissimulation or malingering*. If the defendant's deficits are believed not to be valid, and the defendant's deficits would be minor in the absence of dissimulation or malingering, this interpretive process itself may justify an opinion of competence.

The second class includes cases in which the defendant's deficits are *not related to dissimulation and they are either very serious or very slight.* The deficits will be either extremely consequential or barely consequential regarding the defendant's participation in the trial process. Most examiners, lawyers, and the judge are likely to agree on competence or incompetence, respectively, in these cases.

The third class includes all cases between the two extremes in the second class above. Many of the cases in this chapter are of that type. We know that setting aside extreme cases, no particular degree or type of deficits automatically constitutes competence or incompetence. Once we know the extent of the defendant's deficits, how do we interpret whether that extent or degree of deficit constitutes competence or incompetence to stand trial?

The clues to this interpretation are in the legal definition and purpose of competence to stand trial. Consider the *Dusky* definition:

> [T]he test must be whether he [the defendant] has sufficient present ability to consult with his attorney with a reasonable degree of rational understanding and a rational as well as factual understanding of the proceedings against him.

The examiner has interpreted for the court the "present ability," and the examiner has described the "degree of" rational and factual understanding, as well as reasons for any competence ability deficits. To go from there to the Conclusory objective, we must attend to two key words in the definition: "sufficient" and "reasonable." Deciding "competence" or "incompetence" requires that you interpret whether the defendant's abilities, as you have described them, are "good enough" to satisfy the *Dusky* standard, or whether the deficits are "too serious" to satisfy it.

"Good enough" or "too serious" for what? In Chapter 1 we described the three purposes of the competence standard: to safeguard fairness for the defendant, integrity for the criminal trial process, and accuracy of information for the court. What the examiner is interpreting, therefore, is whether the deficits as described are "sufficient" to ensure a fair trial, uphold the system's integrity, and assure the accuracy of evidence.

There are only two ways to make these interpretations. One is to weigh the evaluation's evidence against one's knowledge of the court's sense of "fairness." The court always applies its notion of fairness when arriving at its conclusions about competence or incompetence. Many examiners can use their experience in their local courts to judge what the court typically has perceived as fair or unfair. What has the present court—the judge—decided in cases like this? The second way is to employ one's own notion of "fairness." What do I believe is fair?

Notice that neither of these approaches to arriving at a competence or incompetence opinion requires any clinical expertise or clinical interpretive process. One nationally recognized forensic psychiatrist, when asked his opinion about competence or incompetence, testifies this way: "Your honor, I do not have an *expert* opinion about that. But I can testify to my *personal* opinion." He means that he has been qualified to testify as an *expert* based on his specialization in clinical psychiatry and its forensic application, not on matters of moral and legal conclusions. His *personal* opinion is based on what he, as an individual, considers to be just and fair.

Some examiners choose not to answer the conclusory question, for reasons explained here. Others, however, do answer "competent" or "incompetent." No further guidance can be offered about how to decide this. It is either a guess about what the court usually finds in such cases, or it is a personal moral judgment about what is fair.

DISPOSITIONAL OBJECTIVE: INFERENCES ABOUT REMEDIATION

The law and traditional competence to stand trial literature have used the term "restoration" to refer to the question of intervention to improve a defendant's capacities for trial participation. This term makes sense if a person's competence deficits are the consequence of an episodic disorder prior to which they had better capacity. Yet many defendants have no former condition representing any better capacities than their present ones. That is typically the case for persons with developmental disabilities (if they have no other mental disorder). It is also true for children or adolescents whose incompetence is due largely to developmental immaturity. There is nothing to "restore," because they were no more mature prior to their present circumstance. Therefore, this discussion refers to interventions with all incompetent defendants as aimed at "remediation" rather than "restoration."

Chapters 1 and 2 indicated that two types of evaluations require Dispositional interpretations. First, if the court concludes that a defendant is incompetent, the court needs information addressing whether the defendant's deficits can be remediated and, if so, what will be required. If the deficits are not remediable, or if they cannot be remediated within the time limits provided by statute, then in many jurisdictions the charges may be dismissed (often followed by civil commitment for care and treatment). If the condition might be remediable, the court needs information to order appropriate intervention to accomplish remediation.

Second, if a defendant is then provided some intervention, the defendant must be reevaluated periodically to determine the degree of progress in the remediation program and to adjust answers to the dispositional questions accordingly.

THE DISPOSITIONAL QUESTIONS

Dispositional interpretations focus on the following questions to assist the court at this stage of the proceedings:

- Are the deficits related to the defendant's incompetence remediable?
- If so, what intervention is most likely to succeed for this defendant?

- Where is that intervention best accomplished?
- Given that intervention, what is the likelihood that remediation will allow the defendant to meet competence criteria?
- Within what period of time is this likely to be accomplished?

Interpreting clinical data to address these questions is somewhat different for adults and adolescents, and examiners should consult more comprehensive resources to guide their interpretations. (For adult defendants: Melton et al., 2007; Zapf & Roesch, 2009. For juvenile defendants: Grisso, 2005; Kruh & Grisso, 2009).

Interpretation initially focuses on the nature of the condition responsible for competence ability deficits and certain baselines for their remediation. For example, defendants whose incompetence is due to *mental illness* are most often restored within about 6 months, often sooner (for adults, reviewed by Melton et al., 2007; for adolescents, reviewed by Larson & Grisso, 2012). Defendants whose competence deficits are due to *developmental disability* are less often remediated sufficiently to attain competence (around 50% for adults and adolescents). Questions about the specific intervention that will offer best prospects for remediation require clinical knowledge of the effects of various interventions, as well as individualized judgments based on clinical information about the specific defendant.

Deficits that are due to *developmental immaturity* appear to have good remediation rates (around 80%-90%, as reviewed by Larson & Grisso, 2012). But this may be due to the fact that many adolescents are found incompetent because of poor Understanding, and they have the capacity to learn what is needed through educational remediational approaches.

Difficult questions are raised, however, when deficits are due to immaturity in cognitive processing of information. Some adolescents, especially if they are 12 to 14 years of age, will not yet have reached the developmental stage that allows them to exercise "formal operations"—the ability to form abstract concepts, imagine future situations one has never encountered, and employ something more than a short-range time perspective in imagining consequences of one's decisions. Before they have developed these abilities, young people are particularly disadvantaged in situations requiring decisions (e.g., pleading, waiver of rights) that have significant long-term consequences. But what type of remediation can create capacities for abstract thought before a young person's brain has sufficiently matured to engage in it? No such remediation is available, although some potentials are being explored (see Viljoen & Grisso, 2007, for a review).

Questions about likelihood of success and the likely time that it will require often focus on the time that the statute allows for remediation of incompetence. In effect, the question is not how long it will take, but whether it is likely to be accomplished in less than the statutory time limit. "Success" is defined specifically as remediation of competence deficits. This objective is not the same as other clinical treatment contexts, in which the aim is to assist the person to function adequately and safely in the community. Many incompetent defendants are eventually found competent even when their conditions have not been remediated sufficiently to constitute "remission" of the disorder or to assure adequate psychosocial functioning in a broader sense.

COMPETENCE REMEDIATION PROGRAMS

Knowing your state's programs for remediation of incompetence is essential for satisfying the Dispositional objective. Most states have such programs, often in secure psychiatric facilities and state programs for persons with developmental disabilities. Some states also have special competence remediation programs for incompetent juveniles. They may be located at inpatient adolescent psychiatric units. States increasingly are recognizing that locating those services in child psychiatric units alone is not appropriate, because many adolescents found incompetent have no need for psychiatric care. States increasingly are developing juvenile competence remediation programs for adolescents that operate in nonpsychiatric settings (e.g., juvenile pretrial detention centers) or while juveniles are living at home with parents. (See Larson & Grisso, 2012.)

Many incompetence remediation programs include not only treatment for defendants' mental conditions, but also special didactic and experiential curricula designed to augment the defendant's Understanding, Appreciation, and Reasoning associated with trial participation. The methods vary from classroom-like instruction and practice to videotape depictions of events in a defendant's adjudication process. Whatever the state's programs, examiners interpretations of remediability will require that they be familiar not only with the nature of the programs, but also with the specific services that the programs provide as well as their quality.

Chapter 6

COMMUNICATING FINDINGS

Preparing a written report is the final step in the process. This chapter offers guidelines for written reports of competence evaluations. Oral expert testimony is required in only a minority of competence cases, but it is very important when it is needed. There is little about testimony for competence evaluations that is any different from testimony for other forensic evaluations. Therefore, those guidelines are not described in this book, but Appendix A provides a number of references where you can find excellent suggestions for forensic testimony in general.

GUIDANCE FOR COMMUNICATION OF COMPETENCE EVALUATIONS

To whom are the results of competence evaluations communicated? This depends on the source of the referral. The most typical referral source is the court itself. If the court has ordered the evaluation, the results should be reported and sent only to the court—that is, the judge or the judge's clerk. The court will then decide how the competence report will be distributed, but typically the court will send it to both the prosecutor and the defendant's legal counsel. If either of them wants your oral expert testimony in a competence hearing, they will communicate this to the judge who will then request your testimony.

Sometimes defense counsel will have contracted with the examiner independently for a competence evaluation. In these cases, the evaluation has been conducted under attorney-client privilege, and the results of the evaluation "belong" to the defendant. In these circumstances, your first communication of the results should go only to defense counsel who will then decide whether the results will be entered into evidence in the case.

Beyond these general guidelines, communication of the results raises special issues associated with the needs and demands of various people who will eventually use the results.

THE COURT

The court will depend on you to submit your written report in a timely fashion according to the amount of time that the court has allowed for the evaluation. It will also expect a report that fulfills the requirements set down by state law or administrative practice (as discussed in Chapter 1). One thing that courts find especially helpful is your use of a uniform outline for your competence reports. Across time, this allows the judge to learn how you organize your reports and, therefore, where to find relevant information in your reports.

It is common in many jurisdictions for courts to order both a competence to stand trial evaluation and a criminal responsibility evaluation at the same time. In these cases, best practice holds that you should write and submit two separate reports for the two referral questions. Criminal responsibility reports address a defense—a plea of not guilty by reason of insanity (NGRI) by the defendant. The evaluation, however, has been ordered before the defendant has decided whether to plead NGRI. Therefore, in most jurisdictions, courts will send the criminal responsibility report to defense counsel only, allowing counsel to decide whether to assert the defense (in which case the report will be used as evidence in the case). Competence reports, however, typically are sent by the court to both defense and prosecuting attorneys. Providing separate reports allows this to be done without submitting the criminal responsibility results to the prosecutor.

Why is this important? Criminal responsibility reports generally include a great deal of information about the defendant's own description of his or her version of the alleged offense and what the defendant was experiencing and observing at that time. This information often is self-incriminating, including admission of various behaviors that could damage a not-guilty defense if that is the way the defendant eventually decides to plead. The use of separate reports protects that information from disclosure to the prosecution unless and until the defendant decides to plead NGRI.

DEFENSE COUNSEL

If you are performing a competence evaluation at the request of defense counsel (not as a court order), it is good practice to discuss the results with the attorney prior to preparing a written report. There are several reasons for this.

First, it gives the attorney an opportunity to determine whether to use the results in a competence hearing. The attorney might decide not to do so, for example, if the results do not support an incompetence finding. In that case, there may be no need for a written report, and both you and the attorney can be spared the added time and cost of preparing one.

Second, competence evaluations sometimes raise other questions of legal or psychological significance. For example, you might have found that the defendant has a serious mental illness that requires attention apart from the question of competence. This is sometimes better addressed in consultation with the defendant's attorney than in a written competence report.

Third, sometimes this pre-report consultation can sensitize the examiner to special problems that might arise in courtroom use of the evaluation findings. The defense attorney might describe to you certain questions that can be raised by opposing counsel to challenge the case. It is not your job to modify your *results* to meet these possible challenges. But sometimes one can better organize the report or decide on how the results should be *worded* when one anticipates these challenges. For example, imagine that you compared the 15-year-old defendant's capacities to those of adults. Defense counsel might tell you that she anticipates that the prosecutor will ask for a comparison of the 15-year-old defendant to the capacities of other 15-year-olds. With this advance notice, you can consider whether you might be able to address this in the report.

THE DEFENDANT

Occasionally, defense counsel asks the examiner to communicate the results to the defendant prior to a hearing. If the evaluation has been done specifically at the request of defense counsel, you should welcome the opportunity to do this. It is consistent with our professional standards that urge us to ensure that examinees receive accurate, understandable, and tactful (nonharmful) information regarding evaluation results. It can serve to prepare the defendant for your courtroom testimony, which sometimes will include mental health labels and terms that the defendant might not understand. Failing to understand them, the defendant might have an adverse reaction to them, all of which might be avoided by a brief session to explain them to the defendant and minimize their potential negative impact.

THE PUBLIC

Examiners occasionally are contacted by news reporters prior to, during, or after cases that attract the interest of the public. This is far less likely in competence cases than in many other types of forensic evaluations. Yet in highly publicized cases, people can become quite interested in the fact that a defendant charged with a very serious offense might "get off" because he is found incompetent without reasonable prospects of remediation. Reporters may request information from the examiner concerning professional observations, reflections, and opinions about the defendant.

As a general rule, you should not communicate the results of your evaluation to anyone but the court or parties in the case prior to and during the legal process of competence adjudication. But some professionals believe that it is acceptable to offer comments to public media *after* the case has been adjudicated, because the legal proceedings are public and your opinions are a matter of legal record at that point.

In contrast, you should consider the following argument to the contrary. At the time of your evaluation, you did not warn the defendant that you might communicate to public media the information that he or she would give you. The interview was not confidential, you told the defendant that the court would know the results, and a court hearing is in the public domain. But you cannot presume that the defendant understood the latter condition. Defendants probably do not expect the results of their evaluations to be discussed before cameras on the courthouse steps. They expected that the results would be used in a legal proceeding.

Therefore, talking about the results in public creates two problems. It breaches the conditions under which you solicited the defendant's information, and it contributes to a general mistrust of forensic mental health examiners. Indeed, it may erode even the faith of the public in the confidentiality of professional-client relationships generally. Most people do not make a distinction between clinicians who do forensic evaluations and clinicians who treat people.

FUNCTIONS OF COMPETENCE REPORTS

Skills that you have learned for writing reports of general clinical evaluations will serve you well for many aspects of reporting the results of competence to stand trial evaluations. Yet a report based only on your general clinical report-writing practices will not satisfy the requirements for a good competence report. They are different from general clinical reports in three important ways: their *legal* demands, their *forensic* demands, and the demands of your *reader*.

COMPETENCE REPORTS ARE LEGAL DOCUMENTS

The competence to stand trial report serves as a legal record to document and preserve the competence evaluation. It archives the examiner's contacts with the defendant, the procedures and methods that were used, the examiners findings and opinions, and the examiner's reasoning for those opinions. The document is legal evidence that establishes facts presented to the court to assist it in reaching a legal decision. As such, it must meet certain requirements regarding its content and form that are different from those that apply to general clinical reports. We will examine these requirements in the following sections of this chapter.

COMPETENCE REPORTS ARE FORENSIC DOCUMENTS

Competence to stand trial reports are driven by a forensic question—the defendant's competence. How the evaluation is designed, what you ask the defendant, and what you describe in the report all follow directly from the definition of competence to stand trial. *Competence reports must not address any legal or clinical questions that were not asked by the court.* The defendant's general clinical needs are relevant only if they help readers understand the defendant's capacities related to competence to stand trial or remediation to correct incompetence.

In this sense, competence to stand trial reports are selective in the data that they report. You may learn a great deal about the defendant's history and personality that you will never describe in a competence report. History and personality data must be reported only if they have a direct bearing on your opinion about the defendant's competence to stand trial.

COMPETENCE REPORTS ARE READ BY NONCLINICIANS

Competence to stand trial reports must be written to communicate to their readers, and most of those readers are not mental health professionals. This influences the style of competence reports. They must be as brief and nonrepetitive as possible, and they must describe your findings in ways that are understandable to nonclinicians. Otherwise they fundamentally fail to communicate, and the best evaluation will be nullified by that failure. More will be said about this when we talk about writing style.

ORGANIZATION AND CONTENT OF COMPETENCE REPORTS

Appendix E provides an example of a competence evaluation report prepared according to the guidelines offered in this book. Competence evaluations may be outlined in many ways, and various jurisdictions have their idiosyncrasies. But competence reports have evolved to have a fairly similar organization across jurisdictions: (a) the referral question and introductory information; (b) the data collection methods used; (c) all clinical data relevant for the referral question; and (d) interpretations and opinions related to the competence question. Many competence reports have four subheadings representing this organization, something like the four subtitles in the following discussion.

REFERRAL QUESTION AND IDENTIFYING INFORMATION

Competence reports begin with a section that states *the source of the referral and the forensic question that the report addresses.* When appellate courts themselves write opinions describing their decisions, they begin by establishing the reason that they have authority (jurisdiction) to hear the case. Similarly, competence reports must begin by establishing the examiner's source of authorization to perform the evaluation (the name of the court and judge, or the name of private counsel). In their own reports of their decisions, courts then identify the legal question they were asked to address. Similarly, your report should clearly cite and state verbatim the legal definition of competence to stand trial, and you should briefly describe your translation of that into the types of abilities that are relevant for addressing that legal question.

Also, it is helpful to include a description of the reasons that the competence question was raised, if you know them. For example, "Mr. Jones' legal counsel expressed having had extreme difficulty communicating with Mr. Jones, as well as making sense of Mr. Jones' reflections on things ranging from his everyday life to the events surrounding his charges."

METHODS OF EVALUATION

The competence report should then offer a section on your *methods for collecting data*. This should provide a detailed listing of all sources of information that you used in the evaluation. It should contain a list of all dates, places, times, and length of time of all interviews with the defendant, attorney, and other third parties. It should contain a detailed list of every document you reviewed. It should include a list of all psychological tests or psychiatric checklists that you administered.

This is also the place for a description of the process that you used to inform the defendant of the purpose of the evaluation. It should describe specifically what you told the defendant about the purpose of the evaluation and the limits of confidentiality. This is not satisfied by writing that you "warned him about the limits of confidentiality." What did you tell him those limits were? You should also describe the defendant's own response when you asked about the defendant's understanding of what you described.

Many examiners also include here a subsection describing anything unusual about the evaluation process that might have a bearing on the results. Examples include the defendant whose mother died between the first and second interview session, or a case in which the psychological testing had to be performed under jailhouse conditions that created enormous distractions for the examinee.

CLINICAL INFORMATION

This section of the report, typically the longest, describes your clinical observations. To the court, these are the observations of a witness—what the witness saw and heard—and constitute the primary evidence for the court's use in its decision making.

When writing this section, there are two important rules. First, *all data relevant for the evaluation should be reported in this section.* Second, *this section should include only observations, not interpretations.* All interpretations, opinions, and inferences are reserved for the fourth (final) section of the report. A test score is an observation; its meaning (e.g., "He is very deficient in his ability to form abstract concepts or ideas") is an interpretation or inference. You *observed* the defendant struggling to make sense of a hypothetical plea agreement, but your *explanation* of why this happened and what it suggests about his capacities as a defendant are interpretations and opinions.

The Clinical Observation section typically has a number of subheadings for reporting relevant observations and data in an orderly fashion. The following is a common set of subheadings for competence reports.

Background and History

Provide information identifying the defendant's history. The most important aspects of a history for purposes of competence evaluations are educational history, health history, mental health history, and criminal justice history. Usually this should be brief. Competence evaluations rarely require detailed chronological accounts of each of the defendant's past arrests, convictions, or hospital admissions. They may require more detail, however, on matters that will eventually bear on the Causal objectives of the evaluation. For example, perhaps your later interpretations of the cause of the defendant's deficits in competence abilities will focus primarily on the defendant's mental illness. In that case, the history might well say more about past diagnoses and courses of mental disorder than might otherwise be needed. If the defendant is an adolescent, typically the report will include more information about early development and current educational performance than might be included in most adult cases.

Mental Status and Current Functioning

This section sometimes is outlined as two parts. One part reports the results of a formal mental status examination if one was given. The other part is a description of anything noteworthy in your general or diagnostic interview with the defendant regarding current or recent functioning. Most relevant are any observations about the defendant's recent behavior just prior to and after arrest, as well as information gathered from the defendant's present setting (e.g., behavior while in jail, in a mental health facility, or in recent interaction with the attorney). Even for these observations, however, you need to note only those behaviors that bear directly on eventual inferences about competence abilities and causes of deficits. For example, the number of times a defendant has assaulted someone while being held in jail awaiting the evaluation may or may not be relevant to include in a competence report. If all it signifies is the defendant's dangerousness, it has little bearing on the forensic question. If it will serve to verify features of the defendant's mental illness, then it should be included.

Psychological Test Results

When psychological tests have been used in the evaluation, their results should be reported as observations, not interpretations. For example, reporting the results of an intelligence test involves recording the summary scores and offering the term that characterizes such scores (e.g., "below average") or the percent of persons who make scores in that range. A statement that the individual "is of low average intelligence," however, is an interpretation and is not appropriate for the Clinical Data section of a competence report. Intelligence test scores alone do not provide conclusions about a person's intelligence. The person might have been putting forth poor effort, testing conditions might have been poor, or the person might have been feigning poor ability. Interpretations of the test score are reserved for the report's Opinions section.

Competence Abilities and Deficits

See the example in Appendix E for reporting competence abilities. This section fulfills the Functional objective of competence evaluations. It describes the defendant's competence abilities and deficits as manifested in the competence interview and from other sources. It tells what the defendant knows, understands, believes, or can do as they relate to trial participation.

The description of competence abilities generally includes several paragraphs, often divided into subsections to organize the observations (e.g., Factual Understanding; Appreciation and Reasoning, Assisting Counsel). You should avoid simply repeating verbatim everything the defendant said to all questions asked in the competence abilities interview. But a few well-chosen examples of the defendant's inadequate Understanding or Appreciation about trial-related matters are typically helpful in communicating the most relevant issues.

OPINIONS AND RECOMMENDATIONS

This section should begin with a brief *formulation* of the defendant's relevant mental, emotional, or cognitive condition. This is the place for a diagnostic opinion regarding the defendant's mental illness, an interpretation that the defendant is developmentally disabled, or inferences about the young defendant's cognitive or psychosocial developmental immaturity. Many examiners also describe exactly how the defendant's symptoms meet the *DSM-IV/5* criteria for that diagnosis.

This is followed by a summary and characterization of the defendant's strengths and deficits in competence abilities (the Functional objective). If there are significant deficits in those abilities, the paragraphs that follow should describe the most likely causes of those deficits (the Causal objective). For the Causal discussion, the mere fact that the individual has a mental disorder (or has a developmental disability or is developmentally immature) is not a sufficient explanation. *You must explain how or why the symptoms of the defendant's disorder are logically related to the competence ability deficits that you have observed.* This causal explanation must also identify any other possible interpretations of the defendant's deficits (e.g., malingering or dissimulation). If you have rejected those alternative interpretations, the text should explain why you did.

This is followed by any interpretations related to the Interactive objective—that is, the significance of the defendant's deficits. For example, if the defendant is highly unlikely to be able to testify in court, the report might comment that whether this is an important deficit will depend on whether there is a need for the defendant to testify in this particular case.

At this point, the report offers a Conclusory opinion ("In my opinion, the defendant is/is not competent to stand trial"), if it is your practice to state such conclusions.

Finally, if there is some chance that the court will find the defendant incompetent to stand trial, this section concludes with information that satisfies the Dispositional objective. It should offer the information to answer the questions in Chapter 2 regarding the likelihood of remediation, as well as the intervention and length of time that might be required to accomplish it.

MATTERS OF STYLE IN COMPETENCE REPORTS

Beyond the organization and content of competence reports, there is a great deal to consider regarding the manner and style of reporting. See Grisso (2010) for the most common errors of style in forensic reports in general. The following comments focus on the process of competence report writing as well as ways to avoid the most common errors.

BE CAREFUL AND DEFINITIVE

The competence report is not a statement of your preliminary findings or casual observations. Write as though you are under oath and will be held accountable in public for every word and thought conveyed in the report. The document must be precise, definitive, and complete, not an "interim" report of impressions or a "clinical note" on the case. Approach the task with the thoughtful consideration and multiple revisions that are more typical in preparing manuscripts for journal publication than in writing clinical notes for hospital files.

FOCUS ON THE REFERRAL QUESTION

Like most examiners, usually you will find that you have acquired a considerable amount of information about the defendant. How should you select what to report? As a general rule, information that you will not need for explaining the defendant's abilities and the reasons for deficits in those abilities should not be included in the report. The competence report usually need not contain wide-ranging descriptions of the defendant's history, development, personality, or symptoms that are found in treatment-oriented reports. Moreover, they will not contain much of the information that would be important for other forensic questions, like risk of violence or criminal responsibility.

The rules for selective reporting of data in a competence to stand trial report are these:

- *Report all information* that is important as a basis for your opinions about the competence evaluation's objectives.
- *Report no information* that is unimportant as a basis for your opinions about the competence evaluation's objectives.

STRIKE A BALANCE ON DETAIL

Beyond selecting what to report, how much detail should be provided about the things that are worth reporting? Should specific scores be given, or merely labels and phrases characterizing their range? Should the defendant's specific answers to competence interview questions be included verbatim, or should only some be offered as examples? Should diagnoses be explained briefly or should every relevant symptom be identified in *DSM* fashion? Should the report lay out every detail of the examiner's logic, or should it use broader brush strokes to indicate only the major inferences?

There is no consensus on these matters. One view holds that considerable detail is needed to meet the accountability obligation associated with legal use of one's reports. An opposite view suggests that the report is almost a "summary" of the examiner's findings, allowing for efficiency and reducing judicial review time. I recommend an approach intermediate between these two views: enough detail to establish important facts and to track essential inferences, yet in the style of a digest rather than a meticulous thesis.

Here are two main things to consider when comparing these options. *First, many cases are determined on the basis of your report alone,* without your oral testimony, when both parties stipulate to the results of your report and the court makes a competence or incompetence finding. To serve that purpose, your report must provide enough detail to reduce the likelihood that either party needs to "challenge" your findings, which they may do if you have not told them enough to allow them to have confidence in your opinion. *Second, the more detail you include, the greater the risk that the message will get lost in the words.* Whatever amount of detail you include, avoid repeating yourself. Repetition needlessly lengthens the report and quickly frustrates the reader.

PUT THE READER IN YOUR OFFICE

While I am writing a forensic report, I imagine that the reader—typically a judge or attorney—is sitting just behind me looking over my left shoulder at the computer screen. This focuses me to write about my evaluation results in a style that is likely to contribute to the reader's grasp of what I am trying to say.

One key to understandability is to write simply. When sentences are longer than about 28 words, shorten them. When a paragraph exceeds about 10 lines, find a way to break it into two paragraphs. Avoid using words with more syllables when words with fewer syllables will do just as well. Why write "utilize" when you mean "use?" Why say that a fact "substantiates" something when "shows" conveys the same thing?

Another aid to understandability is to avoid esoteric words and professional jargon. Words like "plethora" and "paucity" can be found in many doctoral dissertations, but they have no place in competence reports. Courts should be spared words like "comorbid," "loose associations" and "oriented times three;" save them for conversations with your colleagues.

AVOID PREJUDICIAL CONTENT

Prejudicial content includes information or use of words that can bias the reader against the interests of the defendant. An earlier discussion in this chapter warned about the dangers of self-incriminating information. Competence reports should contain nothing that the defendant said in the competence evaluation regarding the alleged offense. Most jurisdictions have laws that protect against the use of such information in later hearings on the allegations. Nevertheless, best forensic practice avoids self-incriminating statements in competence reports as an added protection.

Words that you choose to describe the defendant can have a subtle biasing effect on the reader's perception or image of the defendant. Many words are pejorative when they are used as summary concepts to label a person: psychopath, delinquent, criminal, malingerer, repeat offender. Even seemingly neutral identifiers deserve careful selection. For example, a 15-year-old can be identified in a report as a child, youth, adolescent, juvenile, or young man, each having the potential to influence how the reader "frames" the case in terms of the youth's developmental status.

Sometimes jargon and prejudicial language intersect. Traditional clinical reporting may note that a patient "denied substance abuse." All the notation means is that the patient said he didn't use drugs. In contrast, in legal settings the term "deny" is often used to refer to a defendant's claim that is made in the face of evidence to the contrary. Used in a competence report, the term "denies" may imply to nonclinical readers that the examiner thinks that the defendant is lying.

EXPLAIN, EXPLAIN, EXPLAIN

I performed a review of the most common errors in forensic mental health reports nationwide (Grisso, 2010), many of them competence to stand trial reports. The most common error was offering opinions without sufficient explanations. What were the data and logic for arriving at your conclusion that the defendant was not malingering? What is the actual connection between the symptoms of her mental disorder and her belief that legal counsel will be of no help?

Even when an explanation is offered, often it requires a bit of "teaching" for it to make sense to the reader. For example, imagine a 13-year-old who consistently offers short-range reasons for waiving rights (e.g., pleading guilty—"I don't have to sit through a trial") and never shows any signs of weighing the odds (e.g., the likelihood that he'd be found guilty if he pled not guilty). He also seems unable to imagine what it would be like (the negative consequences) if he were in a juvenile correctional facility for a year. Other data suggest to you that he has not yet reached a stage of cognitive development involving abstract concepts and consequences. If the explanation simply reports that he "cannot yet think in abstractions," this is not enough to allow the court to understand your reasoning. Some brief explanation of "abstract thinking" and its development might be needed. For example, "Thinking abstractly includes the capacity to imagine future things one has not yet experienced and to actually apply them to one's own hypothetical future. This is acquired as one progresses from childhood into adolescence. John's answers to questions about his legal future—as well as results of his intelligence test—suggest that he is delayed in this capacity compared to his peers."

In summary, the functions of written forensic reports, discussed earlier in this chapter, provide guidance for making all of your decisions when writing competence reports. These reports are *legal documents*, requiring a high level of integrity to meet the demands for fairness and accuracy in the adjudicative process. They are *forensic documents* for which everything in the report is focused on addressing a specific forensic question—competence to stand trial—not general clinical questions. And the *readers are nonclinicians*, requiring the greatest care to communicate evaluation results simply and clearly.

Chapter 7

THE CONTEXT FOR COMPETENCE EVALUATIONS

The previous six chapters have described "the basics" for performing competence evaluations—defining the legal question and the forensic objectives, using the best methods to collect data, then interpreting and communicating your findings. The present chapter steps away from the examiner's task and examines the context in which it occurs. This, too, is basic for understanding the task. Competence evaluations are performed in the context of legal procedures and institutions that can enhance or impair your ability to do an adequate evaluation. Understanding how they can do that is an important part of performing evaluations that can meet the standards this book has described. In fact, sometimes forensic examiners find that they must make an effort to *change* the legal context so that they can do their job with integrity. This chapter offers guidance for your interaction with the legal system when performing competence evaluations.

WHERE COMPETENCE EVALUATIONS ARE PERFORMED

Many years ago, most competence evaluations were done in the forensic inpatient units of state mental hospitals. Defendants for whom competence evaluations were needed were transported routinely to such units for a period of time necessary to perform the evaluation. Today, most states continue to have forensic inpatient units available for this purpose, but sites for competence evaluations have become more diverse. A large part of this change has been due to efforts to decrease the costs associated with hospitalization. In addition, sending defendants from jails across the state to a few forensic psychiatric units—and sending examiners from distant state hospitals to courts for their testimony—creates costs in time and transportation. And only a portion of competence examinees are actually in need of inpatient psychiatric care.

Consequently, many states have revised their practices so that often their competence evaluations are conducted in settings other than inpatient forensic units. They occur in jails, in mental health centers, and in juvenile detention centers. Many juveniles for whom the competence question is raised do not need mental health care and are not sufficiently dangerous (or in danger) to require detention center custody while awaiting trial. Therefore, many jurisdictions perform competence evaluations for juveniles in mental health clinics or at juvenile court facilities where youths are brought by their parents. One state (Virginia) claims that it almost never is necessary to perform competence evaluations of juveniles in child inpatient psychiatric facilities.

There is no reason to believe that performance of competence evaluations in non-inpatient settings is any less effective than for inpatient evaluations, and they are far more efficient. Non-inpatient settings like jails, however, will sometimes offer examiners difficult or inadequate conditions for the evaluation, especially when standardized conditions are necessary for psychological testing. It is your obligation to make such settings aware of your need for a reasonably quiet and comfortable setting to perform your evaluation. At stake is the quality of the evaluation for the court's use in its decision making.

HOW COURTS OBTAIN COMPETENCE EVALUATIONS

The great majority of competence evaluations are performed at the request of the court, which often is acting upon motions for a competence evaluation raised by the defense or prosecution. How do courts decide who will perform court-ordered competence evaluations? Court practices for referring competence evaluations to clinicians differ considerably across local and state jurisdictions (Grisso et al., 1994; Grisso & Quinlan, 2005).

Three systems are most common. First, courts in some jurisdictions have arrangements with a *mental health center or* (if inpatient care is needed) *a hospital* in the community, where a staff clinician with special expertise in forensic evaluations conducts the court's competence evaluations. Often these clinicians are on salary at the mental health center or hospital where they are working.

Second, some jurisdictions have established forensic *court clinics* to perform competence evaluations. A court clinic typically includes one or more forensic clinicians who are employed by the court or the state's mental health system specifically to provide competence and other forensic evaluations for criminal or juvenile courts. The clinician goes to the jail, detention center, or any other setting in which the defendant is residing, or the defendant is brought to the clinician's office. Often these clinicians have offices within the court building itself.

Third, many jurisdictions call on private practitioners in the community on a case-by-case basis. Typically the court consults a roster of qualified forensic clinicians who are then called, often on a rotating basis. Clinicians employed in this way often are paid a case-by-case fee or hourly rate.

None of these arrangements is known to be better than the others in terms of quality of the evaluations. But there is some tendency for private practitioner jurisdictions to offer poorer financial compensation for the clinician's work. This runs the risk of clinicians "cutting corners" if the low fee cannot reasonably cover the time needed to do a complete job.

A few states specify that every competence case must be evaluated by more than one examiner. One or two states specify a team of examiners (e.g., a psychiatrist, a psychologist, and a social worker), while others require that two or three examiners must do an independent examination of the defendant in each case. Most states, however, require only one examiner.

HOW EXAMINERS ACQUIRE REFERRAL INFORMATION

Competence examiners sometimes are frustrated by the manner in which courts refer competence evaluation cases. Evaluations are more efficient and helpful when more information is provided on referral than "Please evaluate this defendant for competence to stand trial." Here are some of the ways this arises, as well as ways to alter the situation.

WHY THE QUESTION WAS RAISED

Examiners will be far better prepared to initiate a competence evaluation if the examiner knows why the question of competence was raised. Did the defendant manifest some sort of unusual behavior at arraignment? Did defense counsel encounter some particular problem when first communicating with the defendant? Or was the request not based on observations of any particular problem, but simply because the defendant has a long history of treatment for mental disorders? Courts that offer even a sentence or two about the reasons for making the referral will be doing the examiner a great service. Courts often are willing to provide this on a routine basis if they are made aware of the degree to which it is helpful for the examiner.

INAPPROPRIATE REFERRALS

Two kinds of inappropriate referrals for competence evaluations are becoming less common but still arise from time to time. One of these is the *clinical request in disguise.* Judges often encounter cases in which they believe the defendant is truly in need of a diagnostic evaluation to provide necessary treatment, quite apart from the need for information to address a forensic question. In some jurisdictions, however, judges do not have ready access to general mental health services for defendants, but they can always order hospitalization for purposes of getting a forensic evaluation. Sometimes courts order inpatient competence evaluations not because they are primarily concerned about the defendant's competence to stand trial, but because a forensic evaluation referral is the quickest way for them to get necessary mental health services. This causes forensic examiners to have to collect data and address the competence question unnecessarily. Jurisdictions in which this is done can avoid it by restructuring their regulations so that judges have better access to mental health services for defendants. This reduces the tendency to misuse the competence referral system.

Inappropriate competence referrals also arise in jurisdictions with frequent *dual-purpose evaluations*—specifically, referrals that routinely order both competence and criminal responsibility (NGRI) evaluations together. Some administrators argue that an examiner may as well assess for both purposes when there are questions of mental disorder, because the defendant must be seen by the examiner for the competence purpose anyway. In addition, some courts may presume that questions of competence and criminal responsibility are quite similar in the psychological questions that they raise.

In contrast, these two forensic questions involve very different legal concepts and evaluation methods. Not the least of these differences is that the competence question addresses the defendant's present and future mental condition, and criminal responsibility focuses on the person's mental state at the time of the alleged offense. Certain kinds of clinical data are indeed useful in both types of evaluations. Yet they both require additional and different types of data that cause dual-purpose evaluations to take much more effort and time than evaluations for either purpose alone. So routinely ordering competence and criminal responsibility evaluations together is wasteful. Examiners in jurisdictions with a high proportion of dual-purpose evaluations may wish to make their courts aware of these issues.

GETTING RECORDS

Obtaining records is a routine part of the initial stage of competence evaluations. Examiners usually will need to obtain legal records of current charges and past offenses, records of psychiatric hospitalizations, and sometimes education records. Yet often examiners have difficulty obtaining such information routinely prior to their competence evaluations. Examiners should make known to courts and prosecutors their need for specific types of information from defendant's records and files. In some forensic systems where this issue has been raised, courts have been able to ensure that the court's own records routinely will be sent to the forensic examiner with each evaluation referral.

HOW SYSTEMS CONTROL THE QUALITY OF COMPETENCE EVALUATIONS

There are three general ways in which law and courts influence the quality of competence evaluations. Two of these pertain to state statutes and regulations that are intended to create a minimum standard for competence evaluations. The third is the dynamic process that occurs when examiners' evaluation results are subjected to scrutiny in the trial process.

REQUIREMENTS FOR PROCEDURES AND METHODS

State statutes or regulations often provide directions for the process and methods that examiners must employ in competence evaluations. Procedural directives typically focus on how referrals are received, the time limit for completing evaluations, and how the examiner's results will be communicated to the court. Methods requirements focus on the types of data that must be collected and sometimes the evaluation methods that must be used.

Statutes typically do not require specific tests or tools, although a state's Department of Mental Health regulations sometimes do. States with better regulations do not require that any particular set of assessment methods must be used in all competence cases. Rigid specifications about testing would fail to recognize that some competence evaluations require extensive methods and lengthy inquiry, while others may be performed well with far less effort, depending on the nature of the case. Very different psychological testing might be needed, for example, for a defendant whose psychotic symptoms are readily apparent in a psychiatric interview compared to a defendant with possible neurologically based deficits related to a head injury. Some competence cases require no psychological testing at all. Requirements that are too rigid create inefficiency and the potential for less useful evaluations when examiners must apply the same methods in every case.

QUALIFICATION, CERTIFICATION, AND CONTINUING EDUCATION SYSTEMS

Most states specify that competence to stand trial evaluations must be performed by licensed psychiatrists or by clinical psychologists with doctoral degrees. One state does not allow psychologists to perform competence to stand trial evaluations independently, while a few others have such limits "on the books" but deviate from the regulations in practice.

A substantial number of states now have requirements that examiners can perform court-ordered competence evaluations only if they have met certain state requirements beyond licensing. There are many different ways that states do this, but they all require the examiner to do something that is then recognized by certifying the examiner to perform court-ordered competence evaluations (or forensic evaluations generally). In Florida, for example, private practitioners who wish to be on the local court's roster of competence examiners must attend a number of continuing education workshops provided by the state, after which their availability is recommended to the Florida courts. In Virginia, examiners doing competence evaluations in the state's mental health system must attend annual workshops and submit their reports to periodic review by a panel of state's experts. In Massachusetts, examiners must undergo a series of basic workshops, take a written exam, work for a period of time with a certified forensic mentor, and then submit sample reports to a panel for review to determine readiness to perform competence evaluations independently.

THE TRIAL PROCESS AS QUALITY CONTROL

One of the most interesting features of forensic assessment is the role that it plays in the legal process. Your competence evaluation becomes the focus of a process that is aimed at a fair decision about a defendant's capacity to participate in a defense. The report of your results takes center stage in that process. Those who use the evaluation examine its contents, form opinions about its credibility, and usually pay attention to the logic behind your opinions. In some cases, you will be asked to testify about your evaluation. Whatever your opinion, one party in the hearing will question your results under cross-examination. In some cases, the cross-examining attorney will scrutinize your methods, compare them to those that are considered "standard practice" by your peers and published authorities, raise research findings that seem to contradict your interpretations, and challenge the logic of your opinions.

This process of public scrutiny is itself a system of "quality control." It is an imperfect one, of course, because it depends on the degree to which the attorneys and judges who test your practice are themselves informed about competence evaluations. But its impact can be powerful because of our general desire to do a good job, be perceived as credible, avoid being embarrassed, and continue to get referrals so that we can build our practice. Thus the continuous process of scrutiny of our evaluations by attorneys in the legal process creates a dynamic that motivates us to sustain and increase the quality of our work.

GOING FORWARD

As we conclude this reading of "Just the Basics," it is appropriate to recognize what should come next. What is needed so that you can move beyond knowledge of these basics to put them into practice?

At the beginning of this book, an introduction called "Getting Started" described some steps in the process of learning any clinical activity. First one gains an understanding of the relevant definitions, concepts, and methods for the task. This has been the main intention of "Just the Basics." Then one needs exposure to cases in order to "rehearse" the use of one's understanding when applied to various circumstances. Finally, one needs to do cases with some input by a clinician who is experienced in the activity you want to learn.

How you do this for development of your skills for competence evaluations will depend on your own circumstances. If you are a student in a forensic training program, this process will be built into your training curriculum. If you are employed in a forensic mental health system—for example, a forensic hospital unit or a court clinic—you will have more experienced colleagues around you who can help guide these next steps. If you are an independent professional in private practice, you can arrange to purchase weekly consultation from an experienced forensic professional in your community for a brief period of time. In any of these circumstances, I encourage you to select some of the references in Appendix A for further reading. "Just the Basics" will have given you a good overview to get you started, but you will want to do some advanced reading to prepare you for the more complex issues you will encounter as you proceed.

Once competence evaluations have become a regular part of your practice, you will want to establish some ways to maintain and increase the quality of your work. All forensic mental health examiners are obligated to engage regularly in continuing education activities. Even after you have developed a strong basic foundation and have acquired considerable experience, you must keep up with changes in the field of competence to stand trial evaluations. Laws change, new competence assessment methods are developed, and research provides new empirically-based ways to interpret evaluation data. The field does not stand still, and your practice can become obsolete over time—and will more often be uncomfortably challenged in the courts—if you do not continue to learn.

Continuing education comes in various forms. Workshops, of course, are the most common method, and excellent workshops in various areas of forensic mental health practice are offered several times a year by the *American Academy of Forensic Psychology* and the *American Academy of Psychiatry and the Law.* Yet other methods are equally effective. Some forensic examiners are members of peer-consultation groups that meet monthly to discuss their cases, especially those that offer difficult challenges. Others develop a fee-based arrangement with a forensic colleague in the community whom they can contact for consultation as needed when they encounter an especially challenging case. Activities such as these will help you grow in your capacities and skills, allowing you to build your practice, assist the legal process, and contribute to fairness for persons with disabilities in the criminal and juvenile justice systems.

APPENDICES

Appendix A

ADVANCED RESOURCES FOR COMPETENCE TO STAND TRIAL EVALUATIONS

This appendix provides selected resources for advanced or more comprehensive information on competence to stand trial evaluations. There are also single chapter reviews of the topic in numerous "handbooks" of forensic psychology or forensic psychiatry, only one of which is provided here.

COMPETENCE EVALUATIONS WITH ADULTS

Mossman, D., Noffsinger, S., Ash, P., Frierson, R., Gerbasi, J., Hackett, M., Lewis, C., Pinals, D., Scott, C., Sieg, K., Wall, B., & Zonana, H. (2007). AAPL practice guideline for the forensic psychiatric evaluation of competence to stand trial. *Journal of the American Academy of Psychiatry and the Law, 35*, S3-S72.

A supplement to the AAPL journal that offers a comprehensive and well-referenced review of "legal and psychiatric factors to give practical guidance and assistance in the performance of competence to stand trial evaluations." Represents the American Academy of Psychiatry and Law's recommended best practices, but almost all of the guideline is applicable to forensic psychological practice as well. 280 references.

Zapf, P., & Roesch, R. (2009). *Evaluation of competence to stand trial.* New York: Oxford University Press.

A 210-page comprehensive and well-referenced paperback published in a series of 20 books identified as the "Oxford Best Practices in Forensic Mental Health Assessment Series." Describes relevant legal and forensic concepts, assessment methods, and assessment process for competence evaluations. Represents best practices as endorsed by the American Academy of Forensic Psychology. About 200 references.

Melton, G., Petrila, J., Poythress, N., Slobogin, C., Lyons, P., & Otto, R. (2007). *Psychological evaluations for the courts: A handbook for mental health professionals and lawyers* (3rd ed.). New York: Guilford.

Chapter 6 of this handbook offers considerable depth on various legal, forensic, and conceptual issues in competence to stand trial, although less on performance of the evaluation.

COMPETENCE EVALUATIONS WITH JUVENILES

Kruh, I., & Grisso, T. (2009). *Evaluation of juveniles' competence to stand trial.* New York: Oxford University Press.

A 275-page comprehensive guide published in a series of 20 books identified as the "Oxford Best Practices in Forensic Mental Health Assessment Series." Describes relevant legal and forensic concepts, with special emphasis on developmental issues. Offers guidance for all steps from designing the evaluation to writing the report. This book represents best practices as endorsed by the American Academy of Forensic Psychology. About 375 references.

Grisso, T. (2005). *Evaluating juveniles' adjudicative competence: A guide for clinical practice.* Sarasota, FL: Professional Resource Press.

A 175-page guide that was the first to articulate a developmental logic and process for specialized juvenile competence to stand trial evaluations. Describes legal and developmental foundations, as well as all steps in the evaluation. Developed as a product of the MacArthur Foundation Adolescent Development and Juvenile Justice Research Network's project on juveniles' competence to stand trial. 50 pages of appendices include forms for use in organizing and recording the evaluation, an adolescent mental status exam, and the *Juvenile Adjudicative Competence Interview* (JACI).

RESEARCH RELEVANT FOR COMPETENCE TO STAND TRIAL EVALUATIONS

Grisso, T. (2003). *Evaluating competencies: Forensic assessments and instruments* (2nd ed.). New York: Kluwer Academic/Plenum Publisher.

A conceptual analysis of the components of legal competencies, and a comprehensive research review of instruments designed to be used in competence evaluations, including competence to stand trial.

The *Behavioral Sciences and the Law* series of "Five-Year Research Updates on Evaluations for Competence to Stand Trial."

A series of articles in the journal *Behavioral Science and the Law* providing an inventory and annotated commentary on *all articles published in scientific journals during 1985-2010*, relevant for evaluations of competence to stand trial. The articles in this series:

Grisso, T. (1992). Five-year research update (1986-1990): Evaluations for competence to stand trial. *Behavioral Sciences and the Law, 10*, 353-369.

Cooper, D., & Grisso, T. (1997). Five-year research update, 1991-1995: Evaluations for competence to stand trial. *Behavioral Sciences and the Law, 15*, 347-364.

Mumley, D., Grisso, T., & Tillbrook, C. (2003). Five-year research update, 1996-2000: Evaluations for competence to stand trial (adjudicative competence). *Behavioral Sciences and the Law, 21*, 329-350.

Fogel, M., Schiffman, W., Mumley, D., Tillbrook, C., & Grisso, T. (2013). Ten-year research update (2001-2010): Evaluations for competence to stand trial (adjudicative competence). *Behavioral Sciences and the Law, 31*, 165-191.

JOURNALS WITH FREQUENT ARTICLES REPORTING RESEARCH RELATED TO COMPETENCE TO STAND TRIAL EVALUATIONS

Behavioral Sciences and the Law
Journal of the American Academy of Psychiatry and the Law
Criminal Justice and Behavior
International Journal of Law and Psychiatry
Journal of Forensic Psychology Practice
Law and Human Behavior
Open Access Journal of Forensic Psychology
Psychology, Public Policy and Law

RESOURCES FOR WRITTEN REPORTS AND ORAL TESTIMONY

Brodsky, S. (2012) *Testifying in court: Guidelines and maxims for the expert witness* (2nd ed.). Washington, DC: American Psychological Association.

Conroy, M. (2006). Report writing and testimony. *Applied Psychology in Criminal Justice, 2,* 237-260.

Wettstein, R. (2005). Quality and quality improvement in forensic mental health evaluations. *Journal of the American Academy of Psychiatry and the Law, 33,* 158-175.

Grisso, T. (2010, February). Guidance for improving forensic reports: A review of common errors. *Open Access Journal of Forensic Psychology.* Retrieve from http://www.forensicpsychologyunbound.ws/OAJFP/Forensic_Training_and_Education.html

Appendix B

LEGAL CASES RELEVANT FOR COMPETENCE TO STAND TRIAL

This appendix provides citations and annotated content for the most commonly cited federal legal cases pertaining to competence to stand trial. Not included here are many important state appellate cases that shape local demands for competence evaluations. However, the appendix includes some state appellate cases for juveniles' competence to stand trial. This is because competence assessment in juvenile court is a relatively new concept, and its contours are being shaped largely by state-level court decisions in the absence as yet of federal guidance.

FUNDAMENTAL FEDERAL CASES (CITED IN THIS BOOK)

Drope v. Missouri, 420 U.S. 162 (1975)

"*Bona fide* doubt" (a relatively low standard) is the criterion for deciding whether or not to inquire into a defendant's competence (that is, to raise the question and order an evaluation).

Dusky v. United States, 362 U.S. 402 (1960)

Provides the legal definition of competence to stand trial. Most states subsequently revised their statutes to use the *Dusky* standard, some with only minor modifications in wording.

Godinez v. Moran, 113 S.Ct. 2680 (1993)

"Competence to stand trial" means that a defendant is competent to perform all functions that a defendant might need to perform, including "decisional capacities" such as pleading guilty and choosing to dismiss counsel and represent oneself. Some lower courts had claimed that these critical choices required a "higher level of competence," thus proposing that a defendant could be competent for some functions and not for others. The U.S. Supreme Court in *Godinez* decided to the contrary.

Indiana v. Edwards, 554 U.S. 164 (2008)

The standard for competence to stand trial includes competence to *make a decision* about whether to represent oneself at trial (without legal counsel), but does not include one's competence to *actually represent oneself.*

Jackson v. Indiana, 406 U.S. 715 (1972)

A defendant found incompetent to stand trial cannot be held for treatment indefinitely. Commitment for restoration of competence requires a prospect for restoration within a reasonable period of time, and the defendant can no longer be confined on the criminal charges if competence is not restored in a reasonable period of time.

Wieter v. Settle, 193 F.Supp. 318 (W.D. Mo. 1961)

Offered a list of abilities related to competence to stand trial, frequently cited in legal scholarship on the abilities relevant for competence.

Wilson v. United States, 391 F.2d. 460 (1968)

Amnesia can be a proper basis for a finding of incompetence to stand trial. But it does not necessarily signify incompetence. This depends on the importance that the defendant's recall would have in promoting a fair trial under the circumstances of the case.

OTHER FEDERAL CASES (BUT NOT DIRECTLY RELATED TO EVALUATIONS)

Cooper v. Oklahoma, 116 S.Ct. 1373 (1996)

Incompetence need only be proved by "a preponderance of evidence," not the higher standard of "clear and convincing evidence."

In re Gault, 387 U.S. 1 (1967)

Interpreted constitution to require most of the due process protections for juveniles in delinquency proceedings that are afforded adults in criminal proceedings. Applied Fifth Amendment rights against self-incrimination to juvenile delinquency proceedings.

Riggins v. Nevada, 504 U.S. 127 (1992) and
Sell v. United States, 539 U.S. 127 (1992)

These cases addressed the defendant's right to refuse treatment that might be important for restoring or maintaining their competence to stand trial. Together they affirmed the defendant's right to refuse medication unless it was necessary to restore competence, if there were no other ways to do it, and if it was "medically appropriate."

Sieling v. Eyman, 478 F.2d 211 (1973)

A pre-*Godinez* case in a district federal court that supported the notion that a defendant could be found generally "competent to proceed" but might be found incompetent for specific purposes as the trial progressed (for example, incompetent to plead guilty, incompetent to dismiss counsel).

STATE CASES ON JUVENILES' COMPETENCE TO STAND TRIAL

In re Hyrum, 212 Ariz. 328, 332 (2006)

Incompetence may be found in juvenile cases as a consequence of conditions other than mental disorder or disability (e.g., developmental immaturity).

Timothy J. v. Sacramento County, 150 Cal. App. 847 (Cal. Ct. App. 2007).

Finding similarly to *Hyrum*. "We see no significant difference between an incompetent adult who functions mentally at the level of a 10- or 11-year-old due to a developmental disability [mental retardation] and that of a normal 11-year-old whose mental development and capacity is likewise not equal to that of a normal adult."

In re Carey, 615 N.W.2d 742 (Mich. Ct. App. 2000).

Finding similar to *Hyrum* and *Timothy J.* In addition, recognized that juveniles as a group may have lesser capacities than adults, and adopted a "lower" standard of competence in Michigan's juvenile courts than in criminal court. "[I]n juvenile competency hearings, competency evaluations should be made in light of juvenile, rather than adult, norms... A juvenile need not be found incompetent just because, under adult standards, the juvenile would be found incompetent to stand trial in a criminal proceeding."

Appendix C

WAYS TO DESCRIBE ABILITIES AND TRIAL DEMANDS RELEVANT FOR COMPETENCE TO STAND TRIAL

This appendix describes several ways that competence abilities have been inventoried. Additional ways to conceptualize them are offered in the competence assessment tools described in Appendix D. Also included in the present appendix is a list of ways in which trial demands may vary (related to the Interactive objective used in this book).

WIETER V. SETTLE (1961) LIST OF ABILITIES

This court decision offered a set of abilities to guide courts in competence to stand trial cases. It is offered here for historical reasons. The emphasis of the *Wieter* list rests more substantially on a minimal level of factual understanding than is found in more recent analyses.

> *The defendant must have mental abilities to appreciate his presence in relation to time, place, and things, and his elementary processes must be such that he apprehends that:*
>
> 1. he is in a court of justice charged with a criminal offense
> 2. there is a judge on the bench
> 3. a prosecutor is present who will try to convict him of a criminal charge
> 4. he has a lawyer who will undertake to defend him against that charge
> 5. he will be expected to tell his lawyer the circumstances, to the best of his mental ability (whether colored or not by mental aberration), the facts surrounding him at the time and place (of the alleged law violation)
> 6. there is or will be a jury present to pass upon evidence adduced as to his guilt or innocence of such charges.
> 7. [Later in the written decision]: Further, he must have memory sufficient to relate those things in his own personal manner.

MCGARRY'S COMPETENCY FUNCTIONS (MCGARRY, 1973)

These are the 13 functions that were featured in McGarry's influential monograph on competence to stand trial. The original manual offered sample questions to go with each function, and these are offered below. The questions were not intended to be asked in exactly the same way with every defendant. They were intended merely to reflect the type of information that examiners should be seeking. They are not recommended as the sole questions to be asked in a competence interview.

Performance of the defendant role may require the ability to:

1. consider realistically the possible legal defenses
   "How do you think you can be defended against these charges?"
2. manage one's own behavior to avoid trial disruptions
   "What do you think would happen if you spoke out or moved around in the courtroom without permission?"
3. relate to attorney
   "Do you have confidence in your lawyer?" "Why?"
4. participate with attorney in planning legal strategy
   "Is there anything you disagree with in the way your lawyer is going to handle your case, and if so, what do you plan to do about it?"
5. understand the roles of various participants in the trial
   "In the courtroom, during a trial, what is the job of. . . .?"
6. understand court procedure
   "After your lawyer is finished asking you questions on the stand, who then can ask you questions?"
7. appreciate the charges
   "Do you think people in general would regard you with some fear on the basis of such a charge?"
8. appreciate the range and nature of possible penalties
   "If you're found guilty as charged, what are the possible sentences the judge could give you?"
9. perceive realistically the likely outcome of the trial
   "How strong is the case against you?"
10. provide attorney with available pertinent facts concerning the offense
    "Tell me what actually happened, what you say and did and heard and thought before, during, and after you are supposed to have committed this offense."

11. challenge prosecution witnesses
    "Suppose a witness against you told a lie in the courtroom. What would you do?"
12. testify relevantly
    (Judged by the defendant's speech and behavior during the evaluation)
13. be motivated toward self-defense
    "Suppose the District Attorney made some legal errors and your lawyer wants to appeal a guilty finding in your case—would you accept that?"

GROUP FOR THE ADVANCEMENT OF PSYCHIATRY (GAP, 1974)

The Group for Advancement of Psychiatry, a Committee within the structure of the American Academy of Psychiatry and the Law, issued a 1974 report on competence to stand trial that was very influential in shaping policy and practice standards for forensic psychiatry. It helped develop a professional consensus about the abilities associated with competence to stand trial.

Competency to stand trial may involve the ability of a defendant:

1. to understand his current legal situation
2. to understand the charges against him
3. to understand the facts relevant to his case
4. to understand the legal issues and procedures in his case
5. to understand legal defenses available in his behalf
6. to understand the dispositions, pleas, and penalties possible
7. to appraise the likely outcomes
8. to appraise the roles of defense counsel, the prosecuting attorney, the judge, the jury, the witnesses, and the defendant
9. to identify and locate witnesses
10. to relate to defense counsel
11. to trust and to communicate relevant with his counsel
12. to comprehend instructions and advice
13. to make decisions after receiving advice
14. to maintain a collaborate relationship with his attorney and to help plan legal strategy
15. to follow testimony for contraditions or errors
16. to testify relevantly and be cross-examined if necessary

17. to challenge prosecution witnesses
18. to tolerate stress at the trial and while awaiting trial
19. to refrain from irrational and unmanageable behavior during the trial
20. to disclose pertinent facts surrounding the alleged offense
21. to protect himself and to utilize the legal safeguards available to him

GRISSO'S LIST IN *EVALUATING COMPETENCIES* (2003)

The following is adapted from the original.

Functional ability concepts associated with competence to stand trial include Factual Understanding:

1. that the defendant is accused of a crime
2. that the court will decide on guilt or innocence
3. that the trial could result in punishment
4. of the various ways that defendants may plead
5. that certain sentences are possible (their nature and seriousness)
6. of the roles of various participants in the trial process
7. of the general process of trials

They include also the ability to make decisions that are not distorted by failures to appreciate the significant of what is understood or by difficulties in processing those decisions. Specifically, the defendant has:

8. reasoning abilities sufficient to process relevant information during decision making
9. beliefs about one's own trial process are not distorted by irrational or faulty beliefs
10. appropriately motivated to further one's defense

Defendant must have sufficient ability for consulting and assisting counsel:

11. by understanding that counsel works for the defendant
12. by understanding counsel's inquiries
13. by having the capability of responding to counsel's inquiries to provide relevant information for defense
14. by providing consistent account of events relevant to charges and a defense

15. by managing the demands of trial process (stress, maintaining demeanor)
16. by being capable of testifying if necessary

WAYS IN WHICH DEMANDS OF TRIALS MAY VARY (GRISSO, 1988)

Using the Interactive component of competence, the nature of the demands of a trial process may render a defendant's deficits in competence abilities more or less important for purposes of determining competence to stand trial. Many of these demands increase or decrease the complexity of decisions that the defendant may have to make.

The demands of a trial may vary in a number of ways, including:

1. the complexity and multiplicity of charges facing the defendant. Are several charges being tried separately? Does the charge involve a level of intent?
2. the events associated with the alleged offense. For example, were accomplices involved (who might offer different stories about the alleged offense)?
3. the range of possible penalties for this alleged offense. Does the offense allow for one fixed penalty, several possible penalties, a minimum-maximum sentence, life sentence, or death penalty?
4. the range of types of evidence available to counsel without defendant's report. Were there witnesses or not? Will the factual types of evidence make it easy or hard to raise a reasonable doubt?
5. the simplicity or complexity of the legal defenses available. Might the defense constitute no presentation of evidence? Might the defense require many witnesses or presentation of a wide range of evidence not to be brought forth by prosecution?
6. the necessity for defendant's own testimony. Does adequate defense require defendant's testimony, or is it not essential?
7. the probable length of trial. Will the trial require defendant's attention and self-control for only a few hours, or will the trial involve several days?
8. the probable complexity of trial. Will the trial involve only a few witnesses or many? Will the types of evidence presented be complex or relatively straightforward?

9. the potential of trial to arouse emotion. Is the case one in which the nature of the alleged offense has generated community concern and media interest? Are there relationships between the defendant and the witnesses that suggest an emotionally charged trial process?
10. the qualities of the defense attorney. Is the attorney capable of paying attention to some of the defendant's social or emotional needs in addition to the formal defense? Is the attorney capable of explaining trial events to the defendant as the trial proceeds?
11. the sources of social support for defendant during trial process. Does the defendant have relatives who are offering emotional support? Are they capable of doing so?

Appendix D

OBTAINING INSTRUMENTS TO ASSESS COMPETENCE TO STAND TRIAL ABILITIES

Chapter 3 described six instruments designed specifically to assess an examinee's abilities related to competence to stand trial. The following are references to those instruments and their publishers. There are a number of other competence assessment tools not described in this book. Information about them can be found in a recent book by Zapf and Roesch (2009).

COMPETENCY ASSESSMENT FOR STANDING TRIAL FOR DEFENDANTS WITH MENTAL RETARDATION (CAST-MR)

Everington, C., & Luckasson, R. (1992). *Competency assessment for standing trial for defendants with mental retardation.* Columbus, OH: IDS Publishing Company. www.idspublishing.com

COMPETENCY ASSESSMENT INSTRUMENT (CAI)

Laboratory of Community Psychiatry, Harvard Medical School (1973). *Competency to stand trial and mental illness* (DHEW Publication No. ADM77-103). Rockville, MD: Department of Health, Education and Welfare. [This resource is out of print. It is a monograph reporting a research study by A. Louis McGarry and colleagues. The CAI was contained within the monograph. It may be found in some university libraries.]

EVALUATION OF COMPETENCY TO STAND TRIAL–REVISED (ECST-R)

Rogers, R., Tillbrook, C., & Sewell, K. (2004). *Evaluation of competency to stand trial—Revised professional manual.* Lutz, FL: Psychological Assessment Resources. www.parinc.com

FITNESS INTERVIEW TEST–REVISED (FIT-R)

Roesch, R., Zapf, P., & Eaves, D. (2006). *Fitness Interview Test-Revised: A structured interview for assessing competency to stand trial.* Sarasota, FL: Professional Resource Press. www.prpress.com

JUVENILE ADJUDICATIVE COMPETENCE INTERVIEW (JACI)

Grisso, T. (2005). *Evaluating juveniles' adjudicative competence: A guide for clinical practice.* Sarasota, FL: Professional Resource Press. (The JACI is in an appendix in this book.) www.prpress.com

MACARTHUR COMPETENCE ASSESSMENT TOOL–CRIMINAL ADJUDICATION

Poythress, N., Nicholson, R., Otto, R., Edens, J., Bonnie, R., Monahan, J., & Hoge, S. (1999). *The MacArthur Competence Assessment Tool—Criminal Adjudication.* Odessa, FL: Psychological Assessment Resources. www.parinc.com

Appendix E

SAMPLE REPORT FOR A COMPETENCE TO STAND TRIAL EVALUATION

This is a fictitious report based loosely on a real case. It demonstrates a format and style for reporting a competence to stand trial evaluation. I have inserted some commentary in italics after various sections of the report, summarizing how the content is consistent with report-writing guidance that was provided in Chapter 6. In manuscript form, this report is about 8 pages long, double-spaced. As recommended in Chapter 6, almost all sentences are less than 30 words in length, and no paragraphs are more than 10 manuscript lines. The Reading Ease Index score is at the first-year college level.

EVALUATION FOR COMPETENCE TO STAND TRIAL

Examinee:	Jasper Kasper Male, White, 25 (Birth date: December 4, 1975) Docket #743259
Jurisdiction:	Wessex County District Court, Wessex, MA
Examiner:	Samantha Scarlotti, Ph.D.
Dates of Evaluation:	February 5 to February 25, 2001
Date of Report:	February 25, 2001

I. REFERRAL QUESTION AND IDENTIFYING INFORMATION

Honorable Judge Packer, Wessex County District Court, ordered an evaluation of Jasper Kasper to assist in addressing Mr. Kasper's competence to stand trial. Mr. Kasper is charged with resisting arrest and assault and battery on a law enforcement officer, related to an event on February 2, 2001 at Logan Airport. Mr. Kasper allegedly created a disturbance at a ticket counter and resisted arrest when airport security officers were called to intervene.

Mr. Kasper's attorney, Ms. Tess Thompson, raised the question of competence because she was having difficulty understanding Mr. Kasper's behavior. In her words, he seemed "preoccupied," claimed that counsel did not understand his "calling" (which he would not explain further), and told her that it would probably require "several months to convert her" so that she could represent him properly.

I received the order from Judge Packer's office on February 5, 2001. The order requested an evaluation for competence to stand trial, which is defined in Massachusetts in *Commonwealth v. Vailes*, 360 Mass. 522; 275 N.E.2d 893 (1971):

"The test to be applied in determining the competence of the defendant is whether he has sufficient present ability to consult with his lawyer with a reasonable degree of rational understanding and whether he has a rational as well as factual understanding of the proceedings against him." I am a clinical psychologist certified by Massachusetts' Department of Mental Health to perform court-ordered evaluations in criminal cases.

Notice that Part I very economically identifies the defendant, the jurisdiction handling the case, the basic charges, the referral question, why it was raised, its anchor in the state's legal definition, and the examiner's authority to do the evaluation. In only eight sentences, it satisfies all the legal demands of a document as evidence.

II. EVALUATION METHODS

Contacts with Examinee

Interview, City Jail, February 14, 2001 (2.5 hours)
Including use of the *MacArthur Competence Assessment Tool-Criminal Adjudication*
Psychological Testing, City Jail, February 15, 2001 (1.5 hours)
Minnesota Multiphasic Personality Inventory-2

Records Obtained

Hospital discharge records (June 1998; December 2000),
Edith Nourse Rogers Memorial Veterans Hospital
Review of law enforcement officer's report of arrest on present charges

Collateral Contacts

Telephone conversation with Mr. Kasper's attorney, Tess Thompson, February 10, 2001

Telephone conversation with Kate Kasper, Mr. Kasper's mother, February 15, 2001

Process of Evaluation

I telephoned Tess Thompson, examinee's counsel, on February 10 to alert her that I would be evaluating Mr. Kasper. We briefly discussed her concerns about his behavior. My first interview with Mr. Kasper sought general background information about his past functioning, level of current functioning, and any evidence of mental disorder. Also I assessed his capacities related to the state's definition of competence to stand trial, using both a structured interview instrument and a less-structured interview approach. In a separate session I administered the *Minnesota Multiphasic Personality Inventory-2* to assist in diagnosis. Interview and testing conditions in the jail were adequate.

At the beginning of both sessions, I informed Mr. Kasper that I was a psychologist who does evaluations for courts. Therefore, I was not like other doctors in that I was not there to offer him the medical or psychological help that doctors usually provide. I told him that the purpose of the evaluation was to determine whether he was able to participate in his trial and that I would be asking him questions about his life and what he knows about trials. I told him that the court had ordered the evaluation, that I would be reporting to the court anything that we talked about, and that the court would be giving a copy of the report to his attorney and the prosecutor. I said he could tell me or not tell me whatever he liked, but that I would be writing a report to the court either way. When asked to tell me what he understood about this, he correctly identified what the evaluation was for and that "this will all be going to the judge. I'm glad. He needs to know this."

In Part II, every source of data has been identified, and a brief note about the process describes the examiner's logic for selecting the methods. The "limits of confidentiality warning" is somewhat lengthy; other examiners might not offer this much detail.

III. CLINICAL INFORMATION

Background on the Charges

Mr. Kasper is charged with assault and battery of an airport security officer and resisting arrest. This is said to have happened when Mr. Kasper was attempting to collect from airline ticket agents a boarding pass for a flight to Miami connecting to a flight to Panama in Central America. The agent later told the officers that she tried to explain to Mr. Kasper that there was no such ticket in the computerized reservation records. Mr. Kasper became agitated and insistent, and the agent signaled for a security officer who apparently took Mr. Kasper to a security room and tried to quiet him. While in the room, Mr. Kasper is said to have grabbed a telephone, hit the officer on the head, and left the room. He was apprehended by two officers while he was walking toward the security check-in area.

General History

Mr. Kasper was born in Kansas and moved to the Boston area as a teenager when his family relocated here. He lived with his parents and a younger sister. His father was a construction worker and his mother did part-time work at a laundromat. His mother, Kate Kasper, reports that he had no arrests in his teen years, no mental health services contacts, and that he was "average" in school, obtaining a high school degree. She said he was shy and somewhat reclusive as a teenager: "He didn't give me any trouble—just didn't seem to have any friends to get in trouble with." After high school he joined the navy and worked in "inventory and supplies" at a U.S. Naval Support base in Panama City, Florida.

When he was honorably discharged, he went back home for a few months and then, as his mother reports, "he began sort of disappearing," being away for several weeks on end and then showing up at home from time to time. Mr. Kasper describes getting along by getting paid for odd jobs at a second-hand store run by a local church, living in shelters, and living a rather solitary life during which he avoided close relations with others. He has no previous record of arrests. His mother and he claim that he has not abused substances, and his hospital records have no note of substance abuse.

Mental Health History

Mr. Kasper had two known admissions for inpatient psychiatric services, both for about two months at the Edith Nourse Rogers Memorial Veterans Hospital in New Bedford, MA. These occurred in 1998 and 2000.

Discharge notes described a first-occurrence psychotic episode in 1998, symptoms including disorganized thought, marked decrease in his ability or attention to taking care of himself (getting food, finding shelter), hearing the voice of God, and delusional ideas about what God was calling him to do. The delusional ideas did not involve harm to others, but rather an effort to save others from "sins they don't know they are doing." He responded to antipsychotic medication and was discharged in 55 days. The second admission to the VA described similar symptoms (after having discontinued his medication for several months) and a similar remission in about 40 days. His delusional ideas on the second admission manifested a more grandiose quality focusing him on how he could achieve "world peace."

Mr. Kasper's own descriptions of his past mental health conditions were consistent with these hospital notes. Around the time of the first admission, he describes a growing feeling that he was being called by God to some mission. It began to preoccupy him as he became increasingly sure of it ("as God gave me more and more signs"). He said that by the second admission, he was beginning to act on his beliefs. His medical records explained that this apparently led to some disturbances at shelters that in turn led to his second hospitalization.

This history would not be sufficient to explain the development of the examinee's disorder or to build a good, comprehensive treatment plan designed to improve his functioning in the community. It is appropriate for this evaluation, though, because it provides what is necessary—and only what is necessary—for the opinions expressed later about competence to stand trial.

Mental Status Exam

Mr. Kasper is about 6 feet in height and thin. He was dressed neatly in a jail jumpsuit. He described accurately who he was, where he was, what time it was, and my role in the evaluation and its purpose. His initial approach to me appeared quiet, calm, and somewhat distant, although he invested more energy in our discussion when it proceeded to the events surrounding his arrest. He spoke at a normal rate and volume, but with significant pauses before he spoke, accompanied by staring at the floor then looking up to respond. His responses did not suggest confusion or disorganized thinking; they were related to my questions and sufficiently articulated for me to understand his message.

Mr. Kasper's brow was often furrowed and he frequently rubbed his chin when thinking about his answers to questions. From time to time his speech volume would rise and his tone became more insistent when talking about his legal case, but he maintained good physical control.

He accurately answered several U.S. history questions I posed and questions about what was in the newspapers in the past week. In contrast, he gave vague and poorly formed answers to questions about what people thought of him—for example, questions about how his mother saw his lifestyle, and about how others might see his behavior at the airport as strange or odd.

Mr. Kasper's speech and demeanor especially changed when he described the present mission that he believes God has given him: to go to Panama (the country, not Panama City, Florida where he was stationed) and "unite the world—east and west, north and south—by working from its umbilical." He described the "umbilical" as the Isthmus of Panama and found great significance in the Panama Canal's crossing of it (to form the four directions, and symbolically to represent "the cross on which Jesus died"). He was not sure what he needed to do there, but it had something to do with "systematic creation of a family of God that can flow out in all directions." He said also that God had told him that he must be there by Easter, and he is "aware of" certain people who are trying to sabotage his plan. I asked him how he knew this, and he said "I'm told that I should beware of people who try to smile at me when they are talking to me."

Psychological Testing

Mr. Kasper's scores on the MMPI-2 were significantly high on Scale 8 (Schizophrenia; odd thoughts, social alienation) and Scale 0 (Social Introversion), and somewhat high on Scale 6 (Paranoia; suspiciousness, low trust). He was within normal limits on scales that assist in determining whether examinees are under- or overreporting symptoms or attempting to manage a "good" impression. Indexes of substance abuse in the MMPI-2 were within normal limits.

Competency Abilities

I assessed Mr. Kasper's abilities that are related to the standard for competence to stand trial using two methods. The first involved administering the *MacArthur Competence Assessment Tool—Criminal Adjudication* (MacCAT-CA), which asks the examinee questions about trials, reasoning about pleas, and beliefs about one's trial. The MacCAT-CA has standardized questions (asked of every examinee) based in part around a hypothetical case involving a person accused of a crime, and in part on the examinee's perceptions of his own case might unfold. The second method was a more individualized interview about Mr. Kasper's perceptions of a broader range of issues about his own legal situation.

On the MacCAT-CA, Mr. Kasper's scores on two parts of the tool (Understanding and Reasoning) were not significantly different from research data on persons who usually are found competent. But his score on a third section was in the range of persons who are often found incompetent. That section asks examinees to consider whether the process or outcome of their trials is likely to be any different from that of others with similar charges. It is designed to examine whether irrational or illogical ideas might be interfering with the examinee's perceptions of the trial.

In the more individualized interview about his own circumstances, Mr. Kasper correctly told me the names and nature of his charges. He correctly described the roles of the defense attorney and prosecutor ("represents you, makes sure that your story is heard, works against the prosecutor"), and the judge. He offered simple but basically correct answers to my questions about how a trial works. He was not sure of the usual penalties for his charges, but he told me that it didn't matter because he would not be getting penalized (explained later). He provided a coherent description of his version of relevant events at the airport, and he said that he'd had no trouble describing that to his attorney.

In contrast, Mr. Kasper's description of the purpose and possible outcome of the trial were grossly distorted. His story was expressed logically if one accepts the beliefs that underlie the story. But the beliefs themselves were unusual. He explained that his defense would include "proof" that he was justified "by God" to obtain a free ticket to Panama to begin his mission. He explained that "the judge will either find me guilty or arrange for American Airlines to help me get to Panama." So, "of course, I'm going to plead not guilty" because "once the judge hears what I'm doing, God will give him the message." He said he would not want to plead "not guilty by reason of insanity" because he knew "that means the hospital" and that would interfere with his travel plans.

Mr. Kasper seemed very motivated to give proper attention to matters of his defense ("This is important, we need to set things straight") and he seemed to have confidence in his attorney ("I think she might be able to do it"). But he expressed some concern about her ability to defend him properly without the benefit of indoctrination into the "mission" that he feels he has been given. He acknowledged my suggestion that others might not believe in his mission, but he said that this was merely because it was hard to understand until they "get the full picture."

Notice that the mental status, test data, and competence abilities descriptions are mostly "concrete." They describe data—what the examiner saw and heard. There are some summarizing inferences ("He offered correct answers to my questions about how a trial works"), but little that would be called an interpretation. When inferences are stated ("He seemed motivated...."), usually they are followed by a reference to something observable to illustrate the basis for the inference. Notice also that the delusional content has been described without revealing anything that the examinee said about his actions at the time of the alleged offense.

IV. OPINIONS AND RECOMMENDATIONS

Mr. Kasper appears to have about average to somewhat below average intelligence. He has a mental disorder involving delusions and possibly hallucinations that are related to an irrational, fixed belief about his mission from God. He does not show disorganized speech and his general ability to understand most things around him is relatively sound. But the disorder does seriously impair his functioning in everyday life when he has an episodic recurrence of his disorder. He lacks insight into his disorder during these episodes. He recognizes that his ideas are unique to him, but he does not believe that they are symptoms of a mental illness. These symptoms, and the results of his MMPI-2, are consistent with a diagnosis of Paranoid Schizophrenia. This disorder frequently has its onset in early adulthood, as in Mr. Kasper's case.

It is not likely that he is feigning mental illness or his delusion. Elements of the delusion have been apparent for 3 years, including two psychiatric hospitalizations producing notes that describe similar delusional ideas. Moreover, antipsychotic medication has improved his situation between hospitalizations, suggesting that the ideas about a "mission" are part of a psychotic process, not a fabrication for some legal gain. It is also not likely that his "mission" is a form of dedication found in some religious sects, because his belief is not shared by others. Finally, the results of his MMPI-2 offer evidence that he was not exaggerating his psychiatric condition.

Consistent with the nature of his disorder, Mr. Kasper has little difficulty understanding everyday matters, including how trials work, the roles of participants, pleas one can make, and consequences that a defendant might face. But the delusional beliefs related to his disorder—his "mission" and the prospect that others are trying to sabotage it—seriously impair his ability to apply that understanding to his own situation. It has an impact on how he is approaching his attorney, his decision making about how to plead, his insistence on an illogical defense strategy, and his grasp of the likely outcome of the trial.

The first paragraph offers the diagnosis and explains the data that support the diagnosis. The second considers alternative possible explanations for his symptoms and specifically explains why the examiner rejects them. (As Chapter 6 advises, "Explain, explain, explain.") The third paragraph then summarizes the nature of the examinee's competence ability deficits (Functional objective) and relates them to the mental disorder (Causal objective). This explanation of the connection between competence deficits and the disorder is very brief, but in this case it's all that is needed.

If Mr. Kasper is found competent to stand trial, there are two specific contexts in which his delusional ideas will impact his trial. The first is working with his attorney. He is not resistant to working with counsel, but it seems likely that he will insist that counsel pursue an illogical line of defense (not guilty because motivated by obedience to God, but rejection of an NGRI plea). If he does, that places him in jeopardy because of his irrational belief. Second, if Mr. Kasper needs to (or insists on) testifying himself, his delusional belief is likely to drive his testimony more than the questions he is asked.

This illustrates a way to put the findings into context (Interactive objective). It describes the specific demands of the situation that make his deficits significant. Notice that both observations are "conditional," using the "If this . . . then that" approach described in Chapter 6. Notice also that the paragraph frames these as likely consequences of a finding of competence. This is the examiner's alternative to stating an opinion about competence or incompetence (Conclusory objective). It clearly describes to the court the risks to "fairness" if the defendant is found competent, but defers to the court to decide the conclusion. If the report were written by an examiner who chooses to state a conclusory opinion, this paragraph would end with, "In my opinion, the defendant is incompetent to stand trial."

If Mr. Kasper is found incompetent to stand trial, it is likely that a brief period of medication in a Department of Mental Health forensic inpatient unit will reduce the intensity of his delusional beliefs within about 2 months. This estimate is based on the discharge reports from two previous hospitalizations in the past 3 years. They reported that his psychotic thoughts during similar episodes of disorder decreased substantially in that period of time. The clinical evidence suggests that Mr. Kasper would not need placement in a high-security forensic facility during treatment for his incompetence. He is charged with an assaultive act, but he has no other history of violence, has been on the street for many years without evidence of aggressive acts, and showed no signs of violent behavior in his past hospitalizations.

All essential aspects of the restoration question (Dispositional objective) are answered and explained, including recommendations for degree of security during the restoration process.

Respectfully submitted,

Samantha Scarlotti

Samantha Scarlotti, PhD
Staff Forensic Psychologist
Wessex County Court Clinic
Psychologist License #6724 (Mass.)

GLOSSARY

Adjudicative Competence

Competence to participate as a defendant in the criminal or juvenile court adjudicative process. The adjudicative process begins with arraignment and is concluded with the finding in a sentencing or disposition hearing. Competence to stand trial refers to abilities to perform all essential functions as a defendant at all important stages of the adjudicative process, not just at the "trial" (the hearing to decide the case).

Appeal

When a trial court has reached a decision in a case, a process that either party can use to ask a higher court to rule on whether the legal standards or procedures were applied in error in the trial court. Arguments that the lower court misapplied the law may arise for many reasons (e.g., that the facts did not support the decision; the court was not authorized to hear the case; the court manifested some sort of bias; the court used evidence that should have been inadmissible; the court ignored evidence that should have been considered; the decision violated constitutional protections).

Bona Fide Doubt

Literally, "good faith" reason to doubt. In the present context, refers to having some factual reason to raise the issue of possible incompetence (e.g., observation of the defendant's odd behavior), thus avoiding claims that have no reasonable basis and would delay the trial process unnecessarily.

Developmental Immaturity

Having characteristics or abilities that have not yet reached their adult potential. May refer to any physical, cognitive, psychological, or social characteristics that change through childhood and adolescence until they reach an adult level of development.

Dissimulation
Deception. Any effort to misrepresent oneself for some gain.

Dual Roles
In clinical professions, playing two professional roles in relation to the same individual. In forensic practice, this often arises as an issue of ethics when fulfilling the role of forensic examiner and therapist for the same defendant or patient.

Feigning
A type of dissimulation, applied in this book to a defendant's efforts to appear to have deficits in abilities related to competence to stand trial.

Fitness
A term synonymous with "competence" (to stand trial), used in some states and in Canada, the United Kingdom, and Australia.

Idiographic
In psychology, an approach to describing individuals according to unique features that set them apart from other individuals. Contrasted with a "nomothetic" approach, which describes individuals according to some set of characteristics that individuals share to varying degrees.

Informed Consent
A concept in law and ethics that defines valid, autonomous consent by an individual. Informed consent typically requires that (a) the individual is informed of the conditions to which consent is sought, (b) the individual is competent to make the decision, and (c) the consent is made under conditions that are not coercive.

Jurisdiction
Having the power, right, or authority to interpret the law within a defined area of responsibility. Also used to denote the geographic area (e.g., county, state, federal) or subject-matter (e.g., criminal, civil, juvenile) to which such authority applies.

Least Restrictive Alternative

A legal concept in mental health law, referring to the requirement that treatment mandated by a court must be provided in whatever setting will minimize restriction of the individual's liberty while offering a reasonable prospect of accomplishing the goals of treatment.

Malingering

A type of dissimulation typically referring to an individual's effort, for some personal gain, to appear to have a mental illness.

Nomothetic

In psychology, an approach to describing individuals according to some set of characteristics that individuals share to varying degrees and on which they can be compared.

Prejudice

Engaging in judgments, statements of attribution, or actions that threaten damage to an individual's legal rights or claims.

Remediation

In the context of competence to stand trial, any intervention (or its result) that is intended to alter the capacities of an individual found incompetent to stand trial so that the individual may be found competent to stand trial.

Response Style

In clinical psychology, an individual's pattern of responding to test items or interview questions that may create error in the testing or interview outcome. Examples include acquiescence (selecting answers according to what one expects the examiner wants to hear) and malingering (selecting answers that will create an impression of mental illness).

Restoration

In the context of competence to stand trial, any intervention (or its result) that is intended to restore a person to the person's mental state prior to the present one that caused them to be found incompetent to stand trial, so that they may be found competent to stand trial.

Stare Decisis
The policy of courts to abide by or adhere to principles established by decisions in earlier cases similar to the one in question.

Stipulate
In law, to agree, accept, or assent. For example, legal counsel may stipulate to an opinion offered by an expert in a forensic report, indicating that it is accepted or agreed upon (will not be contested) by counsel.

Subpoena
A formal document that orders a named individual to appear before an authorized body (e.g., a court) at a fixed time to give testimony.

Structured Professional Judgment
A method of design for some psychological assessment instruments that assess an individual's status (e.g., risk of reoffending). SPJ tools are designed to structure the professional's data-gathering with a set of empirically derived items or dimensions and often provides criteria for rating those data, while allowing discretion regarding the manner in which the rated data are used to arrive at an opinion. Typically contrasted with actuarial tools, which provide a summary score classifying the individual using research-based actuarial rules.

REFERENCES

Achenbach, T., & Rescorla, L. (2001). *Manual for the ASEBA school-age forms and profiles.* Burlington, VT: University of Vermont, Research Center for Children, Youth and Families.

American Psychology-Law Society and American Academy of Forensic Psychology. (2011). *Specialty guidelines for forensic psychology.* Washington, DC: American Psychological Association.

Borum, R., & Grisso, T. (1996). Establishing standards for criminal forensic reports. *Bulletin of the American Academy of Psychiatry and the Law, 24,* 297-317.

Butcher, J., Dahlstrom, W., Graham, J., Tellegen, A., & Kaemmer, B. (1989). *The Minnesota Multiphasic Personality Inventory-2 (MMPI-2): Manual for administration and scoring.* Minneapolis, MN: University of Minnesota Press.

Cooper, D., & Grisso, T. (1997). Five-year research update, 1991-1995: Evaluations for competence to stand trial. *Behavioral Sciences and the Law, 15,* 347-364.

Fogel, M., Schiffman, W., Mumley, D., Tillbrook, C., & Grisso, T. (2013). Ten-year research update (2001-2010): Evaluations for competence to stand trial (adjudicative competence). *Behavioral Sciences and the Law, 31,* 165-191.

Frederick, R. (1997). *Validity Indicator Profile (VIP) manual.* Minneapolis, MN: NCS Pearson.

Grisso, T. (1986). *Evaluating competencies: Forensic assessments and instruments.* New York: Plenum

Grisso, T. (1988). *Competency to stand trial evaluations: A manual for practice.* Sarasota, FL: Professional Resource Exchange, Inc.

Grisso, T. (1992). Five-year research update (1986-1990): Evaluations for competence to stand trial. *Behavioral Sciences and the Law, 10,* 353-369.

Grisso, T. (1996). Society's retributive response to juvenile violence: A developmental perspective. *Law and Human Behavior, 20*, 229-247.

Grisso, T. (1997). Juvenile competency to stand trial: Questions in an era of punitive reform. *Criminal Justice, 12*, 4-11.

Grisso, T. (2003). *Evaluating competencies: Forensic assessments and instruments* (2nd ed.). New York: Kluwer Academic/Plenum Publishers.

Grisso, T. (2005). *Evaluating juveniles' adjudicative competence: A guide for clinical practice.* Sarasota, FL: Professional Resource Press.

Grisso, T. (2010, February). Guidance for improving forensic reports: A review of common errors. *Open Access Journal of Forensic Psychology.* Retrieved from http://www.forensicpsychologyunbound.ws/OAJFP/Volume_2__2010.html

Grisso, T., & Appelbaum, P. (1998). *Assessing competence to consent to treatment: A guide for physicians and other health care professionals.* New York: Oxford University Press.

Grisso, T., Cocozza, J., Steadman, H., Fisher, W., & Greer, A. (1994). The organization of pretrial forensic evaluation services: A national profile. *Law and Human Behavior, 18*, 377-393.

Grisso, T., & Quinlan, J. (2005). Juvenile court clinical services: A national description. *Juvenile and Family Court Journal, 56*, 9-20.

Grisso, T., Steinberg, L., Woolard, J., Cauffman, E., Scott, E., Graham, S., Lexcen, F., Reppucci, N., & Schwartz, R. (2003). Juveniles' competence to stand trial: A comparison of adolescents' and adults' capacities as trial defendants. *Law and Human Behavior, 27*, 333-363.

Grisso, T., & Schwartz, R. (Eds.). (2000). *Youth on trial: A developmental perspective on juvenile justice.* Chicago: University of Chicago Press.

Group for the Advancement of Psychiatry. (1974). *Misuse of psychiatry in the criminal courts: Competency to stand trial.* New York: Mental Health Materials Center.

Kruh, I., & Grisso, T. (2009). *Evaluation of juveniles' competence to stand trial.* New York: Oxford.

Larson, K., & Grisso, T. (2012). *Developing statutes for competence to stand trial in juvenile delinquency proceedings: A guide for lawmakers.* Worcester, MA: National Youth Screening and Assessment Project and the John D. and Catherine T. MacArthur Foundation.

Loeb, P. (1996). *Independent Living Scales manual.* San Antonio, TX: Psychological Corporation, Harcourt Brace Jovanovich.

McCann, J. (1998). *Malingering and deception in adolescents: Assessing credibility in clinical and forensic settings.* Washington, DC: American Psychological Association.

Melton, G., Petrila, J., Poythress, N., Slobogin, C., Lyons, P., & Otto, R. (2007). *Psychological evaluations for the courts: A handbook for mental health professionals and lawyers* (3rd ed.). New York: Guilford.

Mumley, D., Grisso, T., & Tillbrook, C. (2003). Five-year research update, 1996-2000: Evaluations for competence to stand trial (adjudicative competence). *Behavioral Sciences and the Law, 21,* 329-350.

Overall, J. E., & Gorham, D. R. (1962). The Brief Psychiatric Rating Scale. *Psychological Reports, 10,* 799-812.

Poythress, N., Bonnie, R., Monahan, J., Otto, R., & Hoge, S. (2002). *Adjudicative competence: The MacArthur studies.* New York: Kluwer Academic/Plenum.

Rogers, R. (2001). *Handbook of diagnostic and structured interviewing.* New York: Guilford.

Rogers, R. (2012). *Clinical assessment of malingering and deception* (3rd ed.). New York: Guilford.

Rogers, R., Sewell, K., & Gillard, N. (2010). *Structured Interview of Report Symptoms-2 (SIRS-2) and professional manual.* Odessa, FL: Psychological Assessment Resources.

Rogers, R., Hinds, J., & Sewell, K. (1996). Feigning psychopathology among adolescent offenders: Validation of the SIRS, MMPI-A and SIMS. *Journal of Personality Assessment, 67,* 244-257.

Sparrow, S. S., Cicchetti, D. V., & Balla, D. A. (2005). *Vineland-II Adaptive Behavior Scales.* Circle Pines, MN: AGS Publishing.

Tombaugh, T. (1996). *Test of Memory Malingering (TOMM) manual.* Toronto, ON: Multi-Health Systems.

Viljoen, J., & Grisso, T. (2007). Prospects for remediating juveniles' adjudicative incompetence. *Psychology, Public Policy and Law, 13,* 87-114.

Widows, M. R., & Smith, G. P. (2005). *Structured Inventory of Malingered Symptomatology professional manual.* Odessa, FL: Psychological Assessment Resources.

Zapf, P., & Roesch, R. (2009). *Evaluation of competence to stand trial.* New York: Oxford University Press.